Preface

This book is designed for all who are interested in the religious education of our children. More especially we have tried to give as much practical help as possible to those teachers in our Primary, Middle, and Secondary Schools who are actively involved in this field whether as specialists or not.

The project is the result of several years' work in what was formerly the Divinity Department and is now the Religious Studies Department at Chester College. Each member of the Department has contributed in some way; each has been engaged in the training of teachers. In addition, several areas of academic interest are pursued within the Department – Biblical Theology with particular reference to the Symbolic Language of Religion; Contemporary Religious Thought and Practice in Europe; the Philosophy of Religion; World Religions; the Nature or Phenomenon of Religion as a whole; and Religion and the Arts.

Although specifically denominational interests can play no part in religious education in our state schools, and, moreover, in our view such an education should include some exploration into the nature of religion itself and the world's major religions, the composition of the work nevertheless represents an exercise in ecumenical fellowship within the Christian tradition. It shows how a real unity can arise through a common need and purpose being appreciated and engendering a response, in this case for the children of our country and those who teach them; for the Anglican, Roman Catholic, Methodist, and United Reformed Churches are all represented through the different members of the team.

I am particularly grateful to my colleagues – Mr Thomas Fawcett, Dean of Academic Studies within the college, the Rev. A. L. Poulton, its chaplain, and Mr N. J. Lemon – for their contributions to the chapters that bear their names. In addition, I wish to record my thanks to the remaining members of the Department – the Rev. R. Way-Rider who has so diligently prepared the Index and has assisted in the designing of the work cards for Scheme 4 in chapter 6, and Mr C. Aslet, who has read the complete typescript and given much encouragement and useful advice. I should like to thank Mr David J. Barratt, of the English Department, who has assisted in the preparation of resource lists from relevant English Literature for some of the schemes in chapter 2, Miss P. E. Croucher, Head-teacher of Harthill County Primary School (ages 5–11), Cheshire, and Mrs Janet M. Ranger, Head of the Religious Education Department at Upton-by-Chester High School (ages 11–18 Comprehensive), who have also read the typescript and made valuable suggestions, together with all the past and present student members of the college who have contributed towards the creation, or have assisted in a realization, of several of the sequences of artistic experiences again in chapter 2. I am also indebted to my wife, Lorraine, Superintendent of the Tilston Methodist Sunday School, who has employed the sequences of artistic experiences approach with her class of 3–13 year-olds, and has contributed some of the material for the Creation example.

Finally, I would like to express my thanks to all those who have supported and helped us in our work, some in specific ways as indicated and acknowledged in the text, others in giving encouragement, advice, and criticisms to our ideas, particularly those whom we have met on Religious Education Conferences and Courses, and with whom we have shared and discussed ideas.

John K. Thornecroft
Chester College (A College of Higher Education)

Contents

Introduction

If we were to look at the history of religion, it would soon become apparent that religion has been expressed and communicated in a great variety of ways. Use has been made of all the available means – stories, poems, the dance, drama, song, music, architecture, painting, sculpture, embroidery, the stained glass window, murals, mosaics, and so on. It would also become clear that what today are called art forms whether in writing or otherwise have been dominant and have preceded propositional and conceptual theology both for expression and communication.

Moreover, most art forms had their beginnings in some form of religious activity. Arts were created for the very purpose of expressing and communicating religion.

From these simple facts we are made aware of the natural affinity between art appreciation and the appreciation of religion.

In our view, the modern religious educationalist should take stock of his methodology in the light of what can be learnt from the history of religion.

Consequently, the purpose of this contribution is to focus attention on those lines of approach which involve seeing religious education as being essentially concerned with experience and the expressions of experience.[1] Particular attention will be paid to the relationship between religion and the arts in religious education,[2] including introducing the nature of religious language in the middle school years.[3] Clearly, in using the arts subject barriers are crossed in this approach, but this particular integration process actually ensures that our religious education is primarily about religion and not something else, as the examples of schemes will show, in a way that the more familiar 'marriage' with the humanities so often does not.

In short, we are concerned with ways of making our religious education more effective, so that it fulfils its prime function, which is to explore the religious dimension of life in such a way that teacher and pupil alike can evaluate for their own lives and thought what they experience, examine, and discover in the exploration process, both teacher and pupil being left with their own integrity. This will involve the pupils acquiring the knowledge, understanding, skills, and attitudes necessary to form a balanced and mature philosophy of life.

The educational justification for working on the lines we advocate has been admirably given elsewhere.[4] We have already sought to justify our approach from the history of religion on the assumption that it is right to learn something of the way in which religious understanding may be communicated at the present time from the ways in which religion has always been communicated in the past. Further justification in terms of more specific examples will be provided in subsequent discussions and the schemes of work themselves in the rest of the book.[5]

For practical convenience we have divided our overall approach into three tasks for religious education: (1) the sequences of artistic experiences approach; (2) learning from the experiences of others, particularly as a way of introducing world religions; and (3) introducing literary religious symbols. Of course, material from the world's major religions can be used within the artistic sequences, as some examples make clear, but we feel that the principles of introducing world religions in the classroom are more easily and appropriately considered within the context of our second task.

Notes

1. An admirable summary and discussion of recent developments and the present position for religious education as a whole will be found in the Schools Council Working Paper No. 36 (SCWP 36), *Religious Education in Secondary Schools*, Evans/Methuen Educational, 1971, the title being misleading in that the book looks at all the relevant questions, deals with basic principles, and points the way towards a philosophy of religious education, applicable for teaching all age ranges. It examines the justification and purpose, as well as the various approaches, for religious education today, and draws attention to the need for making real and worthwhile provision in our teaching programmes for the study of world religions. A fuller discussion with suggestions for schemes of work will be found in Michael Grimmitt's valuable book, *What Can I Do in RE? – A Guide to Modern Approaches*, Mayhew-McCrimmon Ltd, 1973. See also *The Durham Commission's Report: The Fourth R*, National Society – SPCK, 1970.

   More specifically, we should note that Harold Loukes in *Teenage Religion*, SCM Press, 1961, and *New Ground in Christian Education*, SCM Press, 1965, insisted that learning must be through experience, a dialogue between teacher and pupil in the search for the meaning of life. Professor Ninian Smart of the University of Lancaster has not only maintained that religious education is primarily a dialogue with religion and religions, see SCWP 36 – p. 42, and N. Smart, *Secular Education and the Logic of Religion'*, Faber, 1968, but in *The Religious Experience of Mankind*, Fontana, 1971, was concerned to show what it feels like to be an adherent of the faiths he discussed, and this has particular implications for the approach of this contribution, as will be seen.

2. We acknowledge that there has been a welcome increase in the use of the arts in religious education. Especially important in this respect are the books: *Lord of the Dance – An Approach to Religious Education* by V. R. Bruce and J. D. Tooke, Pergamon Press, 1966; *Let There Be God*, an anthology of religious poetry compiled by T. H. Parker and F. J. Teskey, Religious Education Press (Pergamon Group), 1968, in two editions, one of which is illustrated with colour plates and photographs of modern works of art; and *The New Creation – A Dramatic Approach for Integrated Studies* by Christopher Herbert, Religious Education Press, 1971. Clearly, these too are particularly valuable for the approach of this book, which, in turn, however, seeks to provide a rationale and a coherent presentation of the use of the arts for religious education.

3. Again, we would acknowledge that something has already been done in this field, although there seems to be a desire to play with this in secular terms rather than to go as it were to the source of symbolic language in religion. So R. Goldman and his team in the series of booklets and work-cards *Readiness for Religion*, published by Rupert Hart-Davis which are companions for his book of the same title published by Routledge and Kegan Paul, 1965. We would contend that many otiose facts and trivial details of unnecessary 'general knowledge' information have to be worked through before the specifically religious content is reached, nor does enough real understanding of the nature of religious language emerge. To be fair this is what we would expect, of course, from an exercise seen only in terms of making a child ready for religion. It will be clear from our whole approach that we believe it

is possible to do genuine religious education much earlier than many, including Goldman, have imagined, indeed we see a continuity of method throughout the educative process.

Grimmitt, op. cit., rightly balances his existential approach in terms of 'depth themes' with a 'dimensional' approach. Nevertheless, he also sees the introduction of religious symbols and language as being part of the existential approach and maintains that we should look at secular symbols before we can look at religious ones. Whereas we would admit there is value in looking at a few secular examples as one possible starting point, we would argue that the process has been considerably overdone, as in the Goldman schemes, and, moreover, that our aesthetic work in the schools should provide the main spring-board for introducing symbols, since the arts are in themselves symbolic expressions and the transition to specific religious symbols is thus more natural, and is, indeed, easier, than the leap from the secular ones usually employed.

4. M. Grimmitt, op. cit., pp. 15–16, 26–27, 75, 88–113, 117, 145, 146, 152, 186–187, 191, 195. See also in the present work p. 15 below.

5. See also on experience, expression, and communication in religion: E. G. Parrinder, *Worship in the World's Religions*, Faber and Faber, 1961, and 2nd edition, Sheldon Press, paperback, 1974; N. Smart, *The Religious Experience of Mankind*, op. cit. n. 1 above; D. Waters, *A Book of Festivals*, Mills and Boon Ltd., 1970; and the books given in the Bibliography (pp. 128–129 and 130 below) under letters (b) and (d).

Section One
The Sequences of Artistic Experiences Approach

Chapter 1
The Approach

The experiences to be provided in religious education are of two kinds when we think in terms of communication: experiences which the child undergoes himself, and experiences of others from which he can learn. These categories are not distinct, however, in that when we listen to a poem, or sing a carol or hymn, for example, we are undergoing an experience ourselves, but, unless we are the composers of the material, we are also reliving someone else's experience and have the opportunity of learning from it. Conversely, if we are looking at a religious festival, for example, objectively in study terms, there may well be occasions nevertheless when within the study we begin to share the experience through looking at a set of slides or in listening to a record, and so on. We make the distinction for convenience in order that we might have a workable procedure both for this book and in the school situation. As long as this is understood we can proceed in this chapter to consider those experiences which the child undergoes himself, as in the singing of a song, in listening to a symphony or poem, or through taking part in a dance-mime or other dramatic activity, or in a whole sequence of such experiences, with which, in fact, we are really concerned here.

(1) In using this approach we are concerned with feeling, emotions, the impact on the senses with artistic response and expression, and a child's natural capacity for awe, wonder, and instinctive apprehension of the mysterious, making use of all these factors throughout the school years. Indeed, the approach is equally valuable in terms of adult communication, as is shown by the use of artistic presentations, usually with drama as its basis, for religious festivals, particularly in eastern religions. It is also seen in the liturgies of the west, and the recent moves towards employing artistic media in evangelistic work.

(2) The approach itself simply involves exploring an idea like 'Peace' or 'Light', for example, or aspects of a religious festival, and through the use of a sequence of artistic experiences an opportunity for discoveries from the experience of man is given. Christian verse, an agnostic's poem, a story from the world's religions, a Beethoven symphony, a Constable painting, a 'pop' song – all these may find a place in the same sequence. The children, of course, are encouraged in addition to provide original contributions for the sequences, such as prayers, poems, songs, and so on. Clearly too, they will be involved in dramatic activity. A glance at the examples in the next chapter will best clarify the procedure outlined here.

(3) Whereas in a 'life-theme' or 'topic' scheme, or, indeed, in learning from the experiences of others and in introducing literary religious symbols, we must begin with a clearly defined aim for the scheme of work in hand, and many of the individual lessons will have their own aims too, when we use the arts as a route of discovery in exploring a theme, we will not start from a specific aim in the same way. We know the area to be explored, but we do not seek to show or illustrate predetermined ideas. Teacher and pupil alike set out on a real voyage of discovery, though the teacher may after the first voyage on a particular theme know what was discovered then and expect some of the same things to be discovered again. Clearly too, he knows the kind of things he wants the class to look out for to a certain extent, though he should resist the temptation to reveal these before the experiences are provided; he clearly chooses the experiences because they are relevant and appropriate, and he is still involved in very careful planning. Nevertheless, the children may see things he does not as the sequences proceed, or see things in a very different way.

Such a procedure is nearer to a genuine 'self-discovery' approach than the 'so-called' self-discovery approaches of the topic schemes, which really simply provide an alternative to direct instruction, the material coming from books rather than the teacher. Of course, the 'usual' self-discovery method does have value in that it is more beneficial for a child to discover what he can in this way than to be told all the answers. However, what he discovers is nevertheless 'planted', for the books and passages where particular factual information is to be found are provided and the child is directed to study them in order that the aim of the scheme might be fulfilled.

Although, as we have said, the teacher chooses and arranges the material for the experiences, there is no specific aim in terms of 'knowledge' or even attitudes to be fulfilled. The artistic vehicles of communication simply yield what they will. This does not preclude, of course, a thorough discussion on what they have yielded. It is another question, however, whether such a discussion should take place, at least within the context of this approach, for its use would seem to go back on the real intention and spirit of the method in terms of instinctive apprehension and appreciation, while the possibility of a coming discussion may spoil the experiences for some children.

We also have to remember that there are many things we learn in life as a whole that we do not appreciate in terms of their real significance or even understand in a cognitive sense until several years have gone by. Similarly, our approach presupposes that it is right to sow seeds which can blossom at a later period, so that in many cases what is apprehended instinctively at the time of the experiences may not be fully appreciated or understood in cognitive terms, until further experiences or reflections on the material concerned during adult life make such realizations possible.

It is true that from a discussion we could begin to evaluate the effectiveness of the method in respect of the religious insights that are gained at the time, but it is also questionable whether we should seek to make such an evaluation, for what we are trying to evaluate could be seen as the personal business of the children concerned. In any case they will talk about the experiences if they want to, asking questions and giving their impressions. Moreover, even without a discussion we could evaluate in terms of enjoyment, a keynote for both aesthetic and religious appreciation.

On the other hand, there will inevitably be a measure of discussion which takes place naturally in the preparation for an actual presentation, particularly in the working out of a dance or situation drama, for example, and certain religious insights will be revealed in the course of deciding the particular execution of certain ideas in the movement work.

The difference lies in whether the material for parts of a sequence is being presented to the children for them to experience, or is confined to expressions by the children which would not require a discussion for the activities to take place, for example in singing: or whether they are providing those expressions of the insights themselves which make a discussion necessary for the experiences to take place at all, as is often the case in dramatic work.

(4) This approach may be of benefit to the agnostic teacher who is prepared to take his share of religious education with his class, but feels the traditional approach and the various 'topic' approaches are not open to him in all sincerity. It is also equally suitable for the classroom and for worship, and, in fact, its use in worship shows that the assembly provides an occasion for learning. More properly, thinking in terms of a sequence of experiences rather than learning in the traditional sense, the barrier between the lesson and what is right for worship is broken down, and we discover something of the spirit in which the classroom lessons and acts of worship are to be taken, so that in a sense the formal lesson disappears as does the notion of the traditional assembly. Moreover, this approach not only makes it possible for the agnostic teacher to play a part in religious education in teaching terms, but also to attend, and even to play an active part, if he wishes, in the sequences of experiences for worship, without in any sense his presence being a false act of betrayal of his own beliefs or lack of them. He is simply on a voyage of possible discovery.

Similarly, it does not matter (in this context) whether a particular child believes in God or not, for this approach does not force him to accept a belief, but gives him the opportunity of understanding from the inside, as it were, something of the nature of religion. His personal decision regarding belief and commitment can be made on the basis of experience rather than the acceptance of what he is told. The artistic vehicles employed must do their own job of communicating. But clearly, what is communicated can be rejected.

(5) Regarding the selection of our material 'the world is our oyster', or almost! We must beware, however, of always using what is most congenial to us and avoiding what we ourselves do not like, on the one hand, and of always using what we know will be popular for the majority, on the other.

Quite apart from the fact that we have the whole class to consider and minority views and tastes are important, we must beware of currying favour. By all means let us speak to the children in terms they understand, in their own artistic idioms, but let it be for this motive, rather than giving in to the temptations which Jesus himself overcame.

Furthermore, we must widen the children's horizons. Our job after all is to educate. We should seek to use examples from as wide a variety of forms and styles as we can, and try to encourage the children to appreciate what they would normally avoid – for the enrichment of their own lives, while we ourselves should seek to find the value in what we normally avoid also. Thus, if we consider the choice of music, for example, we should make use of the whole range – spirituals, jazz, carols, hymns, symphonies, pop and folk and so on.

It is also important, however, to present excellence before the children. This is not a matter of 'types' of the various arts, but how good a particular example is of its kind. Although a badly written hymn tune or scripture chorus can provide a religious experience and be a genuine vehicle of religious communication, because such a tune is poor musically, 'bad of its kind', we should not introduce it. Clearly, in religious education we should not disparage it verbally, since some of the children may have found such a particular example to have been precious to them at church or Sunday school. We simply avoid the problem because there is no lack of good examples of most of the artistic forms and types of those forms. However, whereas we may feel equipped to judge what is a good symphony or hymn tune, perhaps, many of us will need the children's guidance on what is good pop.

Similarly, the use of visual material is crucial. We should always ensure that our pictures and wall-charts, slides and film-strips, on display round the room or shown momentarily on a screen, help in the process of communication, have something to say in themselves. We should, for example, use reproductions of 'good' art, classical and modern, and avoid the sentimental illustrations of Biblical stories that were produced by publishing houses in the past. We should remember that children have imaginations of their own. If a story is told properly there is no need for pictures in simple illustration terms.[1] An exception in terms of quality, however, may be afforded in the showing of articles used in world religions some of which may appear to us to be anything but beautiful, but which are found in immigrant homes and can be bought in some of our multi-racial cities. Many Hindu figurines, for example, come into this category. We can allow ourselves this exception quite properly when arranging a display for a sequence containing Hindu material. Nevertheless, many of the articles we will show will not give rise to any problem in terms of quality.[2]

What we have said in these last two paragraphs is equally valid for the approach to be examined in chapter 3. Also important for later chapters is the remaining problem on selection which we must now raise and discuss.

How far will the age ranges of the children we teach affect our choice of material? More specifically, how early can we introduce mythological material into the sequences or in infant story-time? How far can we use a carol or hymn with young children if the meaning and significance of the words, and, indeed, sometimes the words as words, are not understood? Similar questions could be asked concerning art and the material for drama.

We can begin by suggesting that with the strictly secondary children, 13 plus, we have no problem in terms of art, music, and dramatic activity, and certainly less of a problem in terms of literature – poems, stories, Biblical passages, and so on, than for other age ranges, provided that the necessary training in religious language has been given in the 8–13 range on the lines to be suggested in chapter 5. The only criterion here is that a teacher may feel that a particular piece of writing is too abstruse in style, lacking in clarity, for the particular class he is teaching. This is not a matter of difficulty over form – myth, parable, or whatever, but only of the handling of the form by a particular author or poet which may make it difficult even for a secondary child to grasp what is being said.

Although we shall comment on the suitability of material for all the age-ranges, our main problems will be with the material for younger children. Four things need to be said at the outset:

(a) The overall criterion must be that the art form and the particular material used must be capable of yielding something for the children we teach, not in terms of concepts, but as we have repeatedly said at least in terms of instinctive apprehension, not necessarily revealing the theological insights we see, but at least revealing something that is important and significant.

(b) The problems of choice of material are the same even if we say that with infants or in a first school we could not use a full sequence of experiences approach, since the children could not concentrate for such a sequence; for the shorter use of the method in terms of story-time, or the singing of a carol, is still to be the same in spirit and carried out with the same intent. We are simply limited in length by the children's capacity for concentration and by the practical skills they have acquired or have not yet acquired.

(c) Nevertheless, we could argue that there is a difference in the severity of the problems when we consider the first school age range as opposed to the 8–13 range. If we use mythological material, for example, with the first school children, they will receive such material before any training in symbolic language is given, but the children in the 8–13 range will at least be receiving such training concurrently with the artistic use of similar material in the sequences. The problems are certainly more acute with the younger children, but, whereas many of the difficulties will be gradually resolved by the training in religious language in the middle school range, particularly concerning literary symbols, such a process will by no means solve all the problems. For the symbolic training takes time. It may be that the complex symbolic form of myth, for example, may not be tackled in the process, shall we say, until a child's twelfth year. If so, we are still left with the problem as to whether to exclude such mythological material from a sequence earlier in the process.

(d) At this stage we cannot automatically assume that we shall arrive at the same answers for all the art forms. Alternatively, at any rate, we may arrive more readily at the answers for some than for others, even if in the long run the answers suggested are substantially the same. In other words, we must examine our problems in terms of each art form in its own right as a vehicle of communication.

(i) *Music*

Considering first music without words, a teacher always has the right to take the view that a particular piece may be too difficult for his class to appreciate on musical grounds. However, there is no problem in using music to suggest a feeling or idea like joy or peace, for example, or to help create the right atmosphere for a particular theme. Our problem is really with music that has been set to words, such as for a hymn or carol. Here, our overall criterion must help us towards some answer.

When selecting music for a Christmas sequence, for example, what is important is that something of the spirit, majesty, mystery, and joy of the festival is conveyed through the singing of carols, or hearing some part of Bach's 'Christmas Oratorio', even though many of the words employed cannot be comprehended by the young. So that, although a young child (indeed, even many adults) can make nothing of words like, 'Lo, He abhors not the virgin's womb', or 'God, very God, begotten not created', for example, it is right that he learns to sing 'O Come All Ye Faithful' and appreciates something of the special nature of the birth of Jesus and something of the glory and majesty of the king born at Bethlehem. Similarly, many carols, dependent on medieval modal harmonies for their effect, can convey something of the mystery and wonder, and the quieter aspects of the event, while others with their dance-like rhythms convey the spirit of joy especially characteristic of this festival, even though in both cases the child will understand verbally only those which tell part of the Christmas story, the story itself being taken at face-value.

In other words, provided the music in itself can convey something that is important and meaningful, and can be enjoyed, then it is right for a particular piece to be used, whether the words are understood or not. The exceptions will be those pieces which may not in themselves achieve these things through the music. This may well apply to several hymn tunes, in which case many teachers will want to avoid those hymns which have words that seem obscure or difficult, if they feel that nothing of what is being conveyed by the words of such hymns is also being conveyed by the music.

(ii) *The Visual Arts*

Again, we must rely on our overall criterion. There would seem to be nothing intrinsically wrong with using a display of good art reproductions to provide 'atmospheric background' for a sequence, provided that the children can at least recognize that they are connected with the theme. There is a chance that they will appreciate something of the beauty of the painting or whatever device is used. It is not necessary for them to understand the symbolism of the pictures displayed.

In study lessons, however, a teacher may wish to make use of such art in looking at the experiences and the expressions of the experiences of others and may want to discuss the symbolism of a particular picture. In which case, of course, he will do this only with the age range he feels appropriate, and not before the middle school years. This does not prohibit, however, the use of the same art work within a sequence on the lines described for children of a younger age.

(iii) *Literature*

Here, the question is more complex, and it would be particularly unwise to give hard and fast rules. Rather we must be content with some pointers towards a solution.

Our main consideration is the use of symbolic stories with younger children. It is necessary, however, to remember that there are many other literary forms that we might wish to use, such as poems, and passages from the Wisdom Literature of the Old Testament, for example, or maxims from the Qur'an, or some Hindu prayers, and so on. Since the whole benefit from these would be derived from the spoken and written word, and moreover depends on understanding what is being said, it is clear that in these cases we have to give some deference to Goldman's point of view and select our material with the child's linguistic and conceptual developments in mind.[3] Bearing in mind our overall criterion, however, even from these forms there will be cases where something can be gained from a selection of certain verses for the younger children from a passage which in its entirety would not be suitable, as in the use of the psalms, for example, in a creation theme (as will be suggested below).

We can now turn to the question of introducing symbolic stories. We have said that the problem for the 8–13s is at least easier, if the symbolic training is underway. If the children are beginning to think symbolically, even though, as we noted, this will not solve all the problems, we need not be afraid of using a form like myth in a sequence before it has been examined more formally and its function is understood, provided our overall criterion applies. If we are sure that the form will be examined within a few years, then we should certainly be prepared to use a myth or miracle story, for example, if it really contributes to our sequence.

Similarly, we should feel equally free to use such a story with infants, if we know that the symbolic training is being given in the middle school where our children will be going, for we can simply think in terms of a logical progression of treatment of our story material.

All this calls for much greater co-operation between teachers in the same school and of different schools, particularly between head-teachers, and emphasizes the importance of using religious education specialists in a consultative capacity in our primary, first, and middle schools, and of the role of county advisers and ministry inspectors in helping overcome the problem.

However, even if such co-operation is not forthcoming, and we are not sure that a particular form will be examined in future years, it is as well to remember that we cannot prevent even very young children from meeting this myth and miracle story material outside school, in Sunday schools, from Bible story books given by relatives, and so on. It would seem better therefore that we find ways of using the material even with infants to help in our overall exploration of the religious dimension of life, than to avoid using such material altogether. Moreover, is it right to deprive the younger children of enjoying these stories as stories? This enjoyment, indeed, is the beginning of the artistic appreciation needed for the eventual understanding of the nature of the religious language involved.

If this line of thought is accepted, our remaining task in this section is to look at some of the ways in which these stories might legitimately be used with the youngest children while minimizing the danger of their being taken too literally, if we can.

The first method, applicable in some cases, is to attempt to capture the spirit of a story without actually looking at its literary form, giving our version and avoiding the literary and scientific problems that might arise. The Genesis account of the Creation (Gen. 1–2:4) provides a classic example for this treatment. The method is to set the whole story in an artistic framework and view it with artistic eyes. We take the basic idea of creation – of order emerging out of chaos – and create with the children a dance-mime on the creation process, not following the pattern of the

Biblical narrative's seven days, but simply portraying the idea of order out of chaos. Such a dance can be supported by the use of verses from the creation psalms, so that the children look at what is created through a poetic form. In addition, the singing of creation hymns is particularly valuable. Through 'All Things Bright and Beautiful', for example, the children join in the expression of praise for some of the wonders in nature that we see in creation, but without automatic commitment being implied or any statements about the order in which things have been created being made.

The second method is to place several literary versions, specially designed for the children or retold by the teacher, from different sources side by side. Again employing our creation example, we can use the Genesis version as one of several ancient creation stories from different parts of the world. In this way the children will see them as stories, and will not be so ready to accept them as presenting literal truth.

Indeed, our Bible story-telling with infants should be in the context of the everyday story-time, not isolated as something special or different from the telling of other stories. It is particularly appropriate when using myths that we see their place alongside the great fairy-stories of the world. It is necessary to observe, moreover, that these fairy-stories, which like the myths deal with tensions of the universe, the themes of light and darkness, and of good and evil, are valuable vehicles for religious education and religious understanding or apprehension, even if they have been written primarily for the entertainment of children, certainly in the last few centuries.

However, we should not regard them as purely infant material. They ought to find a place in sequences for older children and adults. Then there could be a juster estimate of both myth and fairy-tale forms. They are, of course, often regarded by many people as being on the same plane as each other, but for the wrong reason, the function of both forms being misunderstood. They should be seen on the same plane, but because both are rich symbolic forms conveying important truths derived from the experience of mankind. Their advantage over historical narratives is that they provide world-wide and timeless expressions of their truths, without the limitations imposed by the time and space dimensions of history.

Not that these truths are totally at variance with historical truth. There are meeting points between myth and history. The conflict between nations arising in the Biblical story of the Tower of Babel, based on the Babylonian myth, for example, has frightening relevance to our political situations today. The picture-language of the stories in Genesis 2–11 as a whole is concerned with the relationship between God and Man – with Man's pride and disobedience and God's judgment and mercy, and provides a mythological expression of what the Hebrews, in fact, experienced throughout their history, and what every man encounters and has to come to terms with in his own personal history. Above all, the historical events of the cross and resurrection are portrayed in the Book of Revelation in terms of the dragon-slaying motif. This motif, of course, was present in the creation narratives of the Sumerians, Babylonians, and the Hebrews, and is found in the mythology of all world religions, and in legends and fairy-tales like George and the dragon, and Jack slaying his giant by chopping down his beanstalk.

In order to discuss the problems of selection regarding literary material, we have inevitably had to be involved with the nature of the material itself and its theology. We shall need to say more about this in chapters 3 and 5, but in the present discussion we should now go on to comment on the remaining artistic form or group of forms which we will need to employ.

(iv) *Drama*

Our dramatic work with younger children, of course, will be largely based on the story form. We have already seen how through a dance-mime we can capture the spirit of a story. In most other cases, however, our drama will follow the details of a narrative more closely. Similarly, when considering the age ranges as a whole, the choice of material for drama will in the main be dependent on the same criteria that we considered for the selection of literary material, with the additional practical factors connected with the children's capabilities for this kind of work, and the greater scope and freedom possible in handling the dramatic forms for interpreting literary passages and religious ideas with older children. We do need, however, to give some special attention to the use of dance-mime activity[4] and spontaneous or improvised situation drama. For it is not only a question of which material is suitable for a given age range, but also which dramatic forms are most useful for religious education in general, and which of these is most suitable in a particular situation.

In deciding on the type of dramatic activity that may be appropriate for expressing our literary material or ideas in a theme, we should remember that dance-mime has three main advantages for school use over the more familiar plays with words:

(a) In a play (or a 'straight' mime in this case also), unless there is a large number of characters, only a few selected pupils will be actively involved; in dance-mime everyone in the class plays an important part, even if there are some parts to be played by particular people.[5] Moreover, a part can be played by more than one child at the same time, not only through the expediency of having several dances on the same theme or a story going on at the same time in different groups, but also because it is perfectly proper when using this form to reduplicate characters within the same dance pattern. For example, in a dance on the Good Samaritan story (St Luke 10:30–35), there can be more than one Good Samaritan, and several priests and Levites. Such a procedure is even more valid if the idea of the parable is being portrayed in terms of some people showing care while others do not.

(b) In dance-mime there need be no words to be remembered, read, or composed by those taking part in the dramatic activity (as there would be for most actors in a play), though words may be recited or read by an individual or group not taking part in the action itself. This does not preclude secondary children, however, from speaking some words while being involved in the action, if the use of such words would be particularly effective in certain places in a dance, but words are not essential for this form and will often be unnecessary.

(c) A stage is not required for dance-mime; any open space will serve. Limited projects can even be undertaken in the classroom.

There is another difference between the play and 'straight' mime on the one hand, and dance-mime on the other. In the former cases the dramatic action simulates the reality as closely as possible; in dance-mime, however, ideas are often suggested, as they are in ballet. Thus, let us say, for example, that A gives B a present. In a play or 'straight' mime A may take out his wallet and give B a pound note, or go to a drawer, take out a box or parcel and give it to B. In the dance-mime, the two parties would simply approach one another, A raising both hands, placed together palms upwards. He then makes a movement indicating the offering, and B similarly makes a receiving action; but neither need actually touch the other, and no 'prop' is needed. This shows a basic difference between the forms, but the exception in some particular can prove the rule. In some situations, for example, it may be thought desirable, particularly with younger children, to use some props, and some movements demand actual physical contact, as in the holding of hands in a ring. The illustration serves, however, to show that the aim is a piece of acted symbolism rather than a dramatic 'theatre' performance. It will be clear that taking part in such symbolic dramatic activity helps the child appreciate symbolic forms in general and makes the task of introducing him to literary religious language much easier.

Despite the use of dance even with very young children in the example we gave for the creation story of Genesis 1, it is necessary for the children to have experience of music and movement infant work before we can employ the dance form for religious education. In the 7–13 range dances based on stories are usually the most appropriate. What we might term 'tension types' – 'Good and Evil', 'Harmony and Discord', 'Caring and Lack of Caring', for example, unless these ideas are shown through a story, are best left in the main for secondary work, though examples like the creation dance provide exceptions. As we have seen, we might, for example, portray caring and lack of caring with 7–13s by dramatizing the story of the Good Samaritan, following the details of the story in the dance. With older children we may prefer to take only the basic idea of the parable and present the idea in a tension type dance.

Dances based on poems or the more philosophical literary passages, like Ecclesiastes 3:1–12 from the Old Testament Wisdom Literature, with or without a reading of the passage concerned and/or the use of a song, like 'Turn, Turn, Turn',[6] which would be appropriate for the example just cited, are generally best left until the secondary years, simply again, because we are dependent on the children understanding the words of the passage or song employed.

Whatever the stimulus for a dance, the movements will usually be performed in time to the beat or rhythms of suitable music. Sometimes, however, the music will be used entirely to help create the right atmosphere and the dancers will not attempt to keep in step with it, especially when a passage of literature is being read or recited at the same time and the movements are arranged to portray certain lines as they are read. This would be the case in the example given in the preceding paragraph, if the first bars of the song were used to provide a prelude, and the final bars a postlude, to the dance itself, and the body of the song was sung *sotto voce* (or the recording was turned down) while the movements were being executed to correspond with the spoken lines. Incidentally, recorded extracts of music chosen for any dance should normally be prepared on tape, since it is rare to find a record which will fit a dance exactly. Occasionally, within a sequence containing several dances, having one dance performed in silence, or simply accompanied by a tambourine or drum beat, can prove most effective.

Finally, we turn very briefly to spontaneous situation drama. Its use has been found to be particularly valuable with handicapped and deprived children of various ages. Its general use in religious education, however, would seem to be most appropriate for the later secondary years, simply because the children are particularly interested and concerned at this stage, just before they leave school, with moral questions and with facing up to the situations and problems they might meet in everyday living.

Nevertheless, this use of drama could be employed for the expression and interpretation of Biblical events and parables in the middle school years. It would provide the teacher with the opportunity of gaining insights regarding the way in which the children view a particular story, as in their attitude to a miracle story, for example. Do they see it primarily as a story of love or of power? Which aspects appear dominant in their thought as seen in their dramatic work? At all events, improvised drama provides an alternative to the dance form in respect of the portrayal of stories and shares two[7] of the same advantages over the formal play.

It will be clear that the above guide-lines given for the various art forms we might employ represent the personal opinions in each case of the present author. Whatever principles each teacher establishes for himself and whatever he feels is right in practice for his particular class, the approach itself presented in this chapter and the methods advocated in further chapters, of course, are not affected, in the sense that their validity is not dependent on the answers given to the problems of selection.

We must conclude this chapter by turning to the question of the presentation of the material itself. Just as in our choice of material we must endeavour to present excellence before the children, so when using a recording of a poem or a piece of music, or when showing a film or a set of slides, we should ensure that the 'performance' and standards of recording are good and that our equipment is in good order. Equally important is the care we take over the display of visual material and in reading a passage of literature ourselves to the children or in our story-telling.

Similarly, when we are concerned with the children's expression work, we must insist on as high a standard in the execution of artistic skills that we can. Of course, we must also ensure that we do not demand the impossible or allow the training and practice procedure to get in the way of the real purpose behind using the artistic forms or the children's enjoyment. We should judge only on the basis of the capabilities of the particular class and its members, and no one should be deprived from participating in artistic experiences.

In any case, the over-riding rule for children's work is that it must be educationally desirable and valuable. Their artistic work should not be viewed as a 'performance'. In dramatic work, for example, we are not aiming at theatre. There is too much feverish preparation to present a performance which will bring credit on the school, particularly at Christmas time. Certainly, it is good that parents see their children at work, but let them see an educational process and appreciate the point of it all. The artistic work done in music, drama, dance, or painting, in any case, should be through a continuous process and parents should be encouraged to see any part of that process, not just, or even at all, a final 'polished performance'.

Even if a presentation of the work in 'performance' terms is to be allowed in some instances, it is vital that there is also a spirit of inter-communion and inter-communication between the participants, and for this to be possible the 'performance' can only be seen as a culmination of part of the continuing education process.

Many teachers will acknowledge the value of this approach for the festivals. It is necessary to re-emphasize, however, that its use must not be confined to the festivals. The approach should be employed concurrently with the approaches of learning from the experiences of others, and, in the middle school years, with the training in symbolic literary language, throughout the school year. The work for festivals should be seen as part of the total educational process and the approach will be used for these not as a special approach particularly appropriate for them, though this may be true, but as an approach which is normally employed in religious education. Aesthetic work in general is particularly important in this scientific and technological age. It fulfils a vital need in the child's make-up and his education cannot be complete without it. Such a view reinforces what we have said concerning the need for using the approach throughout the school year and throughout a child's school career, as well as providing one educational justification for the approach in religious education.

Finally, problems of space, time, numbers of children, the special problems of the multi-racial school, and of organization in general, will arise. All we can say here is that when the approach is used with the assembly or act of worship in mind, then clearly such an assembly on these lines cannot be held every day. Time is needed for preparation. A few rich experiences, organized in such a way that the needs of all our children are catered for, are better than a daily meaningless attempt at an act of worship. Again, the children should be comfortable in the assembly hall. The experiences must be enjoyed.

Particular ways of solving these problems cannot be dealt with here. They are a matter of the organization in a particular school, the facilities available, the attitude of the staff, and the background of the children. There must, however, clearly be a willingness to overcome the difficulties, however daunting in particular circumstances they may appear to be. The effort and thought involved will be very worthwhile and well-rewarded in terms of the children's education, the enrichment of their lives in general, and their religious education in particular.

Notes

1. If the children visualize the story in a present-day setting, this can be considered an advantage. The only justification for using illustrations as illustrations, and they must be authentic, is when approaching a topic through learning from the experiences of others in study terms, as would be appropriate, for example, in schemes on 'Dress' or 'Buildings'.
2. E.g. Jewish prayer shawls, and Sikh slippers and wedding garlands.
3. R. Goldman, *Religious Thinking from Childhood to Adolescence*, 1964, and *Readiness for Religion*, 1965, Routledge and Kegan Paul.
4. The dance form being of particular importance as a vehicle of expression and communication in many religions, both ancient and living, particularly, e.g. in African tribal religions, Hinduism in India, and Buddhism and Shintoism as expressed in the 'Noh' plays of Japan. For its general lack of use in Christianity and the exception see p. 39 below. On dance in religion see: Balwant Gargi, *Folk Theater of India*, University of Washington Press, 1966; Yasuo Nakamura, *Noh – The Classical Theater, Performing Arts of Japan IV*, Walker/Weatherhill in collaboration with Tankosha, 1971. W. O. E. Oesterley, *The Sacred Dance*, originally Cambridge University Press, 1923, reproduced by Dance Horizons Inc. – an examination principally of dance among the ancient Israelites and the cultures of Old Testament times; C. Sachs, *World History of the Dance*, W. W. Norton, 1937, Norton Library 1963, a thorough survey of the dance forms of the world from the earliest times to the present day, which discusses the nature of the dances and their significance for the cultures of origin. For modern educational dance for religious education see V. R. Bruce and J. D. Tooke, *Lord of the Dance*, Pergamon, 1966. For modern educational dance in general see: V. R. Bruce, *Dance and Dance Drama in Education*, Pergamon, 1965; R. Laban, *Modern Educational Dance* (revised edition), Macdonald and Evans, 1965, and *Mastery and Movement*, Macdonald and Evans, 1950; J. Russell, *Creative Dance in the Primary School* and *Modern Dance in Education*, Macdonald and Evans, 1965.
5. In many dances all the children can play all the 'parts', or two teams can be contrasted with one another or answer each other antiphonally, particularly in portraying ideas or natural phenomena in a literary passage like a psalm. They can also change roles as a dance proceeds. For example, in one possible execution of a resurrection dance, some of the children can form a circle to represent the tomb, while others represent Christ and make a cross shape within the tomb. As Christ rises and bursts through the tomb, the children in the circle move round in two columns from the front, the stone having been rolled away, and take up their positions behind or leading off from the cross (which has moved forward) to form a 'V' shape and thus represent the victory over death.
6. 'To Everything There Is A Season', Ecclesiastes 3:1–8, adaptation and music by Pete Seeger, which can be found in *'Faith, Folk and Clarity' – A Collection of Folk Songs*, edited by Peter Smith, Galliard Ltd, 1967, and on record sung by Mary Hopkin, Apple Records (The Beatles).
7. See pp. 12–13, (a) and (c) above.

Chapter 2
Examples

The examples given in this chapter are simply meant to serve as illustrations of the kind of thing that can be done through the approach advocated in the previous chapter, and provide a few guide-lines for those who are new to this type of work. They should not be regarded as 'blueprints'. The planning of a sequence and the choice of the right material for a particular class or group of classes – in short, the creation of a sequence of artistic experiences – must be essentially the prerogative of the teachers and children concerned.

What is required on the part of the teacher is diligent preparation in terms of discovering what is available in the world of art, poetry, music, Biblical passages and themes, and the literature of world religions, being sensitive to dramatic possibilities, together with being willing to have a go, 'learn by doing', and, of course, making use, as appropriate, of any artistic skills which he, she, or an individual child may possess.

Many of the examples are virtually reports of actual presentations of the sequences, or of sequences on similar themes and lines. It is important to show that the approach has not simply arisen from our learning from the history of religion, though this is true, and is not just a theoretical possibility thought up by a religious educationalist in his study, as a way that ought to be tried. The approach has been successfully employed in some schools, colleges, and in adult situations, though we have stressed that there is a widespread need for a much greater appreciation of the importance of the aesthetic side of education in general, and of the use of the arts for religious education in particular.

(1) The Choice

This first example serves to illustrate the basic idea of the approach and many of the features discussed in the previous chapter. In this case the method is used to express a Biblical theme.

Opening Prayer

(a) The Choice of Man for Others and Self

(i) 'The Streets of London' – folk song – solo with guitar.

(ii) 'Social Injustice' – a dance-mime, with music.

Older children can undertake a 'tension-type' dance here, in which the rich proudly enter and the poor follow in ones and twos, seeking help from the rich. The poor are rejected and become miserable. In time, the rich add to their wealth by robbing from the poor (social system implied here rather than criminal activities in the legal sense), adding insult to injury, while the poor become more dejected, lonely, and degraded in various ways.

Younger children can convey the idea by acting out the Good Samaritan story up to the point where the Samaritan would enter (St Luke 10:30–32). Since he does not, the man set upon by thieves is left desolate – without help – or even dies. (Note that the procedure of shortening a story in this way should only be employed in very exceptional circumstances.) In this case the adaptation of the story serves to show how many suffer because of the sins of others (the greed of the thieves, for example), and how many who do fall on hard times for whatever reason do not get the help or justice they expect from the authorities.

(iii) 'Only Man' – D. H. Lawrence – poem, read by one child or the teacher. (*Let There be God*, op. cit., p. 37)

The whole poem can be used with older children. It may be felt, however, that only the first seven lines would be immediately understood by many 9–13s.[1]

Only man can fall from God
Only man.

No animal, no beast, nor creeping thing
no cobra nor hyena nor scorpion nor hideous white ant
can slip entirely through the fingers of the hands of God
into the abyss of self-knowledge,
knowledge of self-apart-from-god.

The following, written by a 12-year-old boy, could provide an alternative or additional poem:

The Serpent's Speech

Come eat of the fruit to you forbidden;
If you do not, life's truths are hidden.
God knows the tree will open your eyes,
And the privilege of knowledge He denies.

To learn good and evil the truth to see,
Partake of the fruit of the knowledge tree.
Remain in ignorance no more,
Great Power and innocence deplore.

D. L. (12 years)

(iv) 'The Tower of Babel' – a dance-mime, with dramatic music: Man seeks to make himself God, but all that he builds eventually crumbles; men fail to communicate and are at variance with one another.

(v) 'Nobody Knows de Trouble I've Seen' – Negro spiritual – solo and guitar, or sung by several children.

(b) The Choice by God for Man

(i) 'Lord of the Dance' – hymn, arranged by Sydney Carter. Sung by all present.

(ii) 'The Pearl of Great Price' – a parable. St Matthew 13:45–46 is read by one person and is then portrayed through a dance-mime. One way in which this can be done is as follows:

One person, who could be the reader, represents the pearl. The remainder in the group,[2] representing men who will search for the pearl, form a circle. First, they are seen eagerly acquiring the wealth of this world in various ways, and gathering it together in the centre of the circle. When the pearl enters, they cast away this worldly wealth (and in some cases actually destroy it). The pearl comes to the centre of the circle and all reach up to him or her, stretching out their hands and rising up, until finally all touch some part of the pearl or all their fingers touch above the head of the pearl. The dance in this case is done without music.

(iii) 'The Beatitudes' – St Matthew 5:3–12. Choral speaking with one symbolic gesture.

The group then sits in their circle with one member standing in the centre. He or she reads the first half of each beatitude in verses 1–10 and the whole of verse 11, while the group replies antiphonally with the second half of each beatitude in verses 1–10 and verse 12, up to the words ". . . great in heaven'. Verse 12, in fact, is shouted out by the group and on the word 'Rejoice' each member flings out an arm and outstretched hand towards all who are watching, if this is the case, or an imaginary audience.

(iv) 'The Cross and Resurrection' or 'Resurrection' alone,[3] – dance-mime with music, or words, or both, as appropriate.

(v) 'Thine Be the Glory' – hymn, tune Maccabeus, G. F. Handel, sung by all present.

Closing Prayer

Notes

1. This particular scheme as presented here is appropriate for older secondary children with the alternatives for a presentation by 8 or 9–13s. The sequence was, in fact, presented as an act of worship for a College Service by students at Chester College. We should observe that in the case of the music used the age ranges concerned do not affect the choice here, while dance-patterns on the main ideas are also possible irrespective of whether we are considering the middle or secondary children, or the student group. The actual pattern worked in any one case would be appropriate to the group concerned.

2. The sequence as a whole is perhaps more effective when one group is basically responsible for Part (a) and another for (b). In classroom terms, however, it is usually desirable to ensure that the children participate in the activities for both sides of a contrast in order that they might have a better chance of appreciating the possible insights that might emerge.
3. For a suggestion of a possible working see p. 16 note 5 above.

(2) **Appropriate Themes: Some Suggestions**

Joy	Despair	Hope
Light (see, e.g. 3 & 9)	Love (see, e.g. 4)	Forgiveness
Loneliness	Anxiety (Fear)	Rejection
Friendship (Neighbours)	Creation (see, e.g. 5)	The Seasons
Destruction (Strife, War,	Power (Strength)	Peace (Harmony)
Discord)	Man's Destiny (see, e.g. 10)	

Notes

1. Some of these can go together in contrasting sequences, e.g. Hope and Fear, Joy and Despair, Light and Darkness, Love and Hate or Wickedness, War and Peace, etc. In fact, it is often easier to work on these lines.
2. Some themes will be seen to be more appropriate for older children, e.g. Destruction, War, etc., while others could be used for all age ranges from 8 upwards, e.g. Power, Love, etc., though the material and aspects chosen would differ in many cases. As mentioned earlier, the method is applicable to infants, but in terms of short experiences and activities, story-time, and so on, rather than sustained sequences. The Seasons example would make an appropriate theme for this age range.
3. As we saw in the previous chapter, the sequences can, of course, present various view-points and contain material from many sources, including the literature of world religions, poems by agnostics, and secular paintings and music, for example as well as artistic statements from Christian sources. This is particularly illustrated by our next example, for which we simply provide a preliminary list of material from which selections can be made for a sequence on 'Light' for secondary children.

(3) **Light**

(a) Biblical Passages

Pss. 27:1; 119:105; Gen. 1:1–6; St Matt. 5:14–16; St John 1:4–9.

(b) From Christian Literature

(i) 'Lead Kindly Light', J. H. Newman.

(ii) As an effective prose passage: *Readings in St John's Gospel*, William Temple, Macmillan and Co., 1939, First Series, pp. 7–8. Beginning with the final paragraph on p. 7, 'Imagine yourself standing alone on some headland in a dark night', followed by the next sentence up to '. . . through the darkness', the reading continues with p. 8 and the sentence in the second paragraph beginning, 'Take any moment of history . . .' to the end of the paragraph ending with '. . . towards the source of light'.

(c) Extracts and Prayers from World Religions

Number and page references are to *With One Voice – Prayers and Thoughts from World Religions*, edited by Sid. G. Hedges, Religious Education Press – Pergamon Group, 1970.

'Light to the Earth', Jewish Prayer Book, No. 6, pp. 3 and 4; 'The Lamp on a Pillar', Muslim, Qur'an 24.35, No. 16, p. 7; 'The Source of Light', Zoroastrian, Zend Avesta, No. 20, p. 8; 'Light of All Lights', Hindu, No. 42, p. 15; 'Lit from the Same Light', Sufi, Jelaleddin Rumi (adapted), No. 442, p. 160; 'Morning', Hindu, Rig Veda, No. 227 b, p. 78.

(d) Music

'2001 Space Odyssey'; 'The Light of the World', from *Godspell*, Stephen Schwartz and John-Michael Tebelek; 'Morning', from *Peer Gynt Suite*, E. H. Grieg; 'Break Forth, O Beauteous, Heavenly Light', chorale from *Christmas Oratorio*, J. S. Bach; from the *Messiah*, G. F. Handel, Nos. 9–12: 'O Thou that Tellest Good Tidings to Zion'; 'For Behold, Darkness Shall Cover the Earth'; 'The People that Walked in Darkness'; and 'For Unto Us a Child Is Born'.

(e) Paintings

The Angelus, Jean Millet, a couple at sunset, the beauty of light; *The Fighting Téméraire*, Joseph Turner, the contrast of the light of the sunset and the darkness of the sea-battle; *The Light of the World*, Holman Hunt.

(f) Dance-mimes

(i) Tension types: 'Light and Darkness', 'Light dispelling Darkness', 'Jesus the Light', etc.
(ii) Story: 'Healing of the Blind Man', cf. St Matt. 9:27–30; St Luke 7:21; 18:35–43.
(iii) The Resurrection.
See also this theme worked in terms of the 'Festivals of Light' – Divali (Hindu and Sikh), Chanukah (Jewish), Christmas (Christian), example 9, pp. 34–35.

(4) Love

(a) Wickedness and Love

A Wickedness
(i) Bible Reading: St Matthew 26: 1–5 and 14–16. The first section read by one child, and the second by another. The passages convey wickedness against Jesus. In this day and age people are still acting in this manner against their fellow men.
(ii) Music: 'Alas for You' from *Godspell* – a recording.
(iii) Dance-mime: Parable of the Wicked Servants – St Matthew 21:33–42.
(iv) Reading: Ps. 139:21–24, by one of the children. Man's conduct against God.
(v) Painting: *Christ driving out the Money Changers from the Temple*, El Greco, enlarged and shown on a screen at this point for a few moments.
(vi) Hymn: 'When I survey the Wondrous Cross'. A sombre hymn of Man's inhumanity to Jesus and to other men.

B Love
(i) Bible reading: St Mark 12:28–34 (cf. Deut. 6:5 and Lev. 19:18), read by three children, 'Love God and Love one another'.
(ii) Music: 'My Sweet Lord', recording by George Harrison, or sung by the children.
(iii) Dance-mime: 'The Good Samaritan', St Luke 10:30–37.
(iv) Poem: 'St Martin and the Beggar', Thomas Gunn. The poem depicts the love of man for his fellow man, and the way of life can be enriched by loving and by sharing what little we have. It could be read by twelve children, each reading one verse.
(v) Sculpture: Reproduction of *The Brother's Kiss*, by Madrassi, enlarged and shown at this point for a few moments on a screen to depict Family Love. A mother is holding her infant son, while her toddler son stands as tall as he can to kiss his brother.
(vi) Hymn: 'God is Love' or similar material.
(vii) Conclusion: Choral reading: St John 3:16–17. 'God so loved . . .'

The above sequence, suitable for 8–13s, was conceived in terms of the Christian tradition. The following further material could be used in a sequence on 'love', including some extracts from world religious literature:

(b) Love

(i) Biblical passages: Pss. 42:8; 116; Ruth 1:1–18 (or 3–17); Micah 6:8; St. Matthew 5:39–44; St John 10:11–18; 15:12–17; 1 Cor. 13:1–13; 1 John 4:18–21.
(ii) Hymns: 'Love divine, all loves excelling', 'The King of Love, my Shepherd is'; 'There is a green hill'; 'Lord Jesus Christ' (Living Lord).

Younger children's hymns: 'I am very glad of God, His Love takes care of me'; 'I love God's tiny creatures'.

(iii) Music (general): Folk songs: 'The Family of Man' and 'If I had a hammer', Pete Seeger and Lee Hays, from *Faith, Folk and Clarity*, op. cit.; 'I don't know how to love Him', from *Jesus Christ Superstar*, Lloyd Webber; Extracts from Tchaikovsky's *Romeo and Juliet*.

Records: 'Goodbye to Love', The Carpenters; 'You've Got a Friend', Carole King, from the L.P. *Tapestry*; 'All You Need Is Love', The Beatles; 'How Can I Tell You?', Cat Stevens.

(iv) Paintings: *The Betrothal*, Franz Haals; *The Woodman's Daughter*, John Everett Millais; *The Meeting*, Charles Blackman; *Love Lesson*, François Gillet (available on a poster); *Home from Work*, Arthur Hughes; *The Virgin Adoring the Child*, Correggio; *St Martin and the Beggar*, El Greco.

(v) Poems and Literature in general: 'The Effort of Love', D. H. Lawrence; 'Two Loves Only', from Michael Quoist's *Prayers of Life*; 'Journey of the Magi', T. S. Eliot – love shown in the effort and hardship – 'we would do it again'; 'People Hide Their Love', Wu Tii Emperor of Liang Dynasty, from *Plucking the Rushes, An Anthology of Chinese Poetry*, compiled by D. Holbrook; 'A Wedding Sermon from a Prison Cell', from *Letters and Papers from Prison*, Dietrich Bonhoeffer, Fontana paperback edition, 1959, pp. 148–150, ending with '. . . death do us part'. Extracts from: *The New Being*, Paul Tillich, SCM Press, 1956, Part I – 'The New Being As Love', pp. 3–59. From *With One Voice*, op. cit.: 'The Greatest of These Is Love', Sufi, Jelaleddin Rumi, No. 346, pp. 127–128; 'All People', Bahai, Baha'u'llah, No. 402, p. 147; 'God, My All In All', Hindu, Dadu, No. 17, p. 7.

Some of the above material will be seen to be more appropriate for upper secondary pupils.

(5) Creation

(a) Artistic Vehicles and Methods

Dance-mimes, choral speaking (e.g. psalms), singing of hymns, readings from poetry and extracts from world religions material, story-telling or reading; in addition the children could 'create' a frieze on order out of chaos, or a 'Creation' model, derived from a dance-mime on the theme or based on the scientific theories of evolution, for which various art materials could be used, and which could provide the visual, background display; they could also write poems, prayers, and hymns of praise and thanksgiving for the sequence.

(b) Material and Resources

(i) Dance-mimes on one or more of the creation myths from Genesis and world religions, ancient and living, or the idea of creation – order from chaos.

(ii) Music: Several creation hymns are available, e.g.: 'All things bright and beautiful'; 'The spacious firmament on high', Joseph Addison (words) – if not used as a poem; 'O Worship the King'; 'Praise, O Praise our God and King' or 'Let us with a gladsome mind'; and Harvest hymns in general.

Extracts from J. Haydn's oratorio, 'The Creation'; L. van Beethoven, Symphony No. 6 in F Major, Op. 68 ('Pastoral'); and 'Creation's Hymn'; Gustav Holst's *Planet Suite*; E. H. Grieg, 'Morning' from *Peer Gynt Suite*; M. P. Mussorgsky, *Night on the Bare Mountain,* particularly valuable for the 'order out of chaos' dance-mime; '2001 Space Odyssey'.

(iii) Literature

Biblical: Gen. 1–2:4, provided other versions from world religions, etc., given also – certainly for 8–10-year-olds; for young children cf. also *Why the World Began*, Pamela Egan, Church Information House, 1973, and David Kossoff, *Bible Stories Retold*, Collins-Fontana, 1968, 'In the Beginning', pp. 11–13 (note the use of humour); Psalms: e.g. 8; 19:1–6; 24:1–2; 29; 50:1–6; 65; 84:3; 89:5–13; 93; 96:10–13; 104:1–30; 135:5–7; 136:1–9; 148; Job 38; Amos 5:8–9; Isaiah (i.e. 2nd Isaiah cs. 40–55) 40:3–5 and 12–24; 41:17–20; 45:12; 55:10–11. See also 'Creation', James Weldon Johnson, in *Let There Be God*, op. cit., p. 16.

World Religions: from *With One Voice*, op. cit.: 'There Is One God', Sikh, Japji (mool Mantra), No. 3, p. 2; 'Light to the Earth', Jewish Prayer Book, No. 6, pp. 3 and 4; 'Lord of Light', Zoroastrian, Zend-Avesta, No. 8, p. 4; 'True Parent of All Things', Chinese, No. 10, p. 5; 'Him Who Is the Uncreated', Bahai, Baha'u'llah, No. 18, p. 8; 'O Lord Creator', Muslim, No. 19, p. 8; 'In the Beginning', Hindu, Rig Veda, No. 22, p. 9.

(c) Creation myth material from various religions will be found in:

Ancient Near Eastern Texts, ed. J. B. Pritchard, Princeton University Press, 2nd edition, 1955; *Hindu Mythology*, Veronica Ions, Paul Hamlyn, 1967; *New Larousse Encyclopaedia of Mythology*, introduced by Robert Graves, Paul Hamlyn, 1959, new edition 1968; T. Fawcett, *The Symbolic Language of Religion*, SCM Press, 1970, pp. 110–113.

(6) For Michaelmas and Harvest*

A report by Mrs I. E. Flanagan, a teacher from Uppermill, Nr Oldham, of a sequence of experiences performed at a Rudolf Steiner school by secondary children of all ages. The two ideas fused together here arose out of the calendar, Harvest festivals taking place around Michaelmas. At the same time, we do have in this example the successful fusion of two basic important ideas: the provision for our bodily needs and our response in thanksgiving, together with provision for our spiritual needs expressed through the 'dragon-slaying' motif.

---

* For another 'Harvest' idea see *Harvest Assembly for Schools – Seeds of Hope* prepared jointly by Christian Aid (P.O. Box No. 1, London SW1W 9BW) and CEM (2 Chester House, Pages Lane, London N10 11R) (copies free), 1974, including artistic and world religion resources.

(a) The children entered in procession to music, bearing harvest gifts. The last child, wearing a chef's hat, carried a loaf of bread ready for the oven.

(b) The Lord's Prayer was sung in Latin by older children (15–16s) as the bread was placed ceremoniously into the oven.

(c) This was followed by a linking speech concerning the need for fire to bake the bread, which led into a dramatic rendering of the Prometheus story.

(d) A further linking speech related the gift of fire from the gods to the terrible fire of a dragon's breath.

(e) The children formed a circle and sang, 'The Knight and the Lady', enacting the story as it unfolded:

> A knight and a lady went riding one day,
> Out into a forest away, away.
> 'Fair knight', said the lady, 'I pray you, take care.
> This forest is evil, beware, beware'.
>
> A fiery red dragon they spied in the grass,
> The lady wept sorely, 'Alas, alas'.
> The knight slew the dragon, the lady was gay,
> They rode on together, away, away.

(f) The song was then repeated, while three children representing the characters of the knight, the lady and the dragon, entered the circle and performed the actions.

(g) Following this, the older children spoke and sang some poems in chorus: e.g.:

> Night is past and day is dawning,
> Wake my soul to greet the morning;
> In the starlit pools of sleep
> Thou hast bathed and drunken deep,
> Gathered strength for this new day,
> Strength to learn and work and play.
>
> If there's danger I can meet it,
> If a battle I can greet it;
> Powers of Darkness cannot fright me,
> Nor the sword of evil smite me;
> For I wear the armour bright
> Of St Michael, God's own knight.
>
> I will fight with my might,
> I will strive to be brave;
> For I've Michael beside me
> To lead and guide me;
> I'll fight for the right
> To be free.

(h) Then, a dance-drama was performed depicting the making of bread, with twisting and wringing movements for the kneading process. From four independent circles, weaving in and out, one large circle was formed.

(i) Throughout the sequence, the bread was baking in the oven and filling the air with a delicious aroma. It was finally taken from the oven, again with due ceremony, to the 'Pater Noster', and was carried at the end of the recessional from the hall.

(7/8) For Christmas

Of course, there is a place for the traditional mime on the Nativity for infant and junior children, and the familiar carol services in schools of all kinds. However, variety is important too. Just as the various themes we can consider appropriate at Christmas time can add so much to the traditional Christmas story, such as looking at customs in other European countries,[1] at festivals of light in world religions,[2] and considering what it is like to have no Christmas in under-developed countries where there are millions without enough to eat, for example, so there are many ways in which we can also use our approach of working through sequences of experiences to enrich this particular festival. Two examples of the kind of thing that can be done are given here.

Notes

1. See *Christmas Customs*, N. F. Pearson, Ladybird Books, 1973; *Stories of Our Christmas Customs*, Ladybird Books, 1964; *Days of the Year*, J. McLellan, REP, 1971.
2. See example 9, pp. 34–35 below.

(7) A Christmas Sequence

The basis of the structure is formed by the use of dramatic activity. We can, for example, have two contrasting dance-mimes. The first concerns the first creation – a creation with power through the might of God. The second portrays the beginning of the second creation in stillness and quiet with the birth of the Saviour, unobserved except by the Holy Family, a few shepherds, and in the gospel story the wise men. The sequence can be lengthened by a third drama, either a dance-mime on light overcoming the darkness, reflecting St John 1:1–14 or Isa. 9:2, 6–7, or a play or improvised drama on the nativity in a modern setting, or, with older children, something on the cross and resurrection, showing that the real meaning of Christmas is to be found in these events.

The dramatic activity will be supported with music, poems, and short passages from the Bible. There is a wealth of material to choose from.

Carols and hymn carols and the negro spiritual 'Mary had a Baby, Yea, Lord', can be sung, while from recorded music extracts from J. S. Bach's *Christmas Oratorio*, the first part of G. F. Handel's *Messiah*, and *A Christmas Cantata* by

Geoffrey Bush are appropriate examples. In addition, some of the pieces from Benjamin Britten's *Procession of Carols* could be sung by older children, or any of the carols can be presented on record for the various age ranges.

With older children any of the poems in 'Let There Be God' (op. cit.) in the section 'I bring you good tidings of great joy', pp. 57–69, can be considered, such as 'Journey of the Magi', T. S. Eliot, 'Bethlehem', Phyllis Hartnoll, 'Three Christmas Trees', Terence Tiller, 'Epstein's Madonna and Child', Geoffrey Dearmer, and 'A Week to Christmas' from 'Autumn Journal', Louis MacNeice. In addition, Thomas Hardy's poem, 'The Oxen', provides a short interesting look at the Nativity scene by one who has lost his faith but wishes he could believe again, as shown in the line, 'hoping it might be so'.

For younger children the following will be useful: 'Christmas Day', Andrew Young, from *The Oxford Book of Verse for Juniors*, edited by J. Britten, 1957; 'Keeping Christmas' and 'Joseph Fell A-Dreaming', E. Farjeon, from *A Puffin Quartet* (of poets) edited by E. Graham, 1958; and from *A Book of 1000 Poems*, edited by Arthur Mee (Evans Brothers, 1942); 'I Will Keep Christmas', P. A. Ropes; 'Christmas', Mary Osborn; 'A Child's Christmas Carol', C. Chaundler; 'He Came So Still' (carol), 'A Christmas Wish', Rose Fyleman; 'A Christmas Verse', 'Kay', and 'Christmas Night', B. E. Milner.

(8) Christmas Celebration

Here, we provide an account of the use of the approach by adults, spanning a wide age range.* At the same time, an examination of the material employed will show that the main idea behind the sequence and much of the material itself would be appropriate for both the 8–13 and the secondary age ranges.

The drama was largely improvised with only the basic ideas being in any sense scripted. The singing, unaccompanied throughout, was provided by the choir, the carols being arranged in two (SA) and three (SSA) parts for the purpose, with the exception of the opening piece and 'O Come, O Come, Emmanuel', which were considered as effective and complete enough sung in unison.

Individual members of the choir, and the choir in chorus, read the passages from the Old Testament prophets, taken from Alan Dale's *Winding Quest*, OUP, 1972, version of the Old Testament and the Revised Standard Version for Isaiah 9:2 and 6, while the later readings were based on ideas expressed in the sequence already with the additional 'Easter' note, and on St John 1:1–14 (RSV). In addition, a narrator read the poems and the two passages from St Luke (RSV and RSV adapted).

For each prophetic passage the drama group 'froze', each member remaining in exactly the same position that she had reached in her secular activity. Time stood still. The present century stopped and we went back in time to the prophets' proclamations of God's Word. Yet, at the same time, within the sequence, it is clear that their message was intended to be relevant for today.

* Performed by the Tilston Women's Institute Drama Group, under the direction of Mrs Sue Peacock, and the Tilston Ladies' Choir under the direction of the present writer for Christmas 1974, Tilston being a village near Malpas, Cheshire. The youngest members taking part were sixth form girls, and the oldest were in retirement years.

Item	Drama	Narr.	Choir
1	Members enter one after the other from the back of the hall, dancing, carrying holly and singing with the choir. They form into a group.	Enters with the drama group. Takes up a permanent position.	Carol: 'Deck the hall with boughs of holly'.
2	Words about Christmas thrown from one to the other, ending with, 'Christmas is coming the goose is getting fat . . .'.		
3	Group freezes.		Speaker 1 (Amos) and Sp. 2 (Deutero–Isaiah): 'Listen to the voice of God.' Sp. 3 (God) 'Far too long have I held my peace, Saying nothing, holding myself back' (fr. 2 Isa.) 'Hold to me if you want to be really alive!' (fr. Amos) Choir: 'Hold to God if you want to be really alive!' (refs. Dale op. cit., pp. 289, 243).
4	Group portrays secular aspect of Christmas, e.g. parcel wrapping, setting up decorations, meal preparation, etc., – a different aspect for nos. 4, 6 and 8.		
5	Group freezes.		Sp. 4 (Jeremiah): 'These are God's words.' (fr. Jer.) Sp. 3 (God) 'If a man falls down he gets up again, If he loses his way he finds the track again, My people have wandered from the road – Why don't they find their way back? Come home, my people, come home! Are you in two minds still?' (fr. Jer.) (refs. Dale pp. 275 and 281).
6	Group portrays secular aspect of Christmas.		

7	Group freezes.	Sp. 4 (Jer.) 'God promised' Sp. 3 (God) 'In the days that are to be I will renew the relationship with man . . . I will make a new covenant with all people, My way will be clear to everybody's conscience. I'll forgive them the wrong they've done – their disloyalty shall be a thing of the past.' (Jer. 31:31–34) (ref. Dale p. 282).
8	Group portrays secular aspect of Christmas.	Sp. 5 (Isaiah of Jerusalem) 'The people who walked in darkness have seen a great light; Those who dwelt in a land of deep darkness, on them has the light shined.' (Isa. 9:2 RSV).
9	Group freezes.	Choir: 'For to us a child is born; to us a son is given; And the government will be upon his shoulder, And his name will be called "Wonderful Counsellor, Mighty God, Everlasting Father, Prince of Peace".' (Isa. 9:6 RSV).
10	Group move to Narr. as if round town crier.	Narr. (Decree): 'In those days a decree went out from Caesar Augustus that all the world should be enrolled: and all went to be enrolled, each to his own city.' (St Luke 2:1, 3 RSV.)

Item	Drama	Narr.	Choir
11	Group move off grumbling except Mary and Joseph who move to centre of rostrum.		Hymn: 'O Come, O Come, Emmanuel' (one verse in unison).
12	Group become Bethlehem — people go about everyday tasks — Mary and Joseph ask, 'How far is it to Bethlehem?' and receive the answer 'Not very far'.		
13	Group mime everyday life in Bethlehem. Mary and Joseph travel enquiring at various houses if there is room. At end of singing by choir enquire at final inn — receive answer 'You can sleep in the stable'.		Carol: 'O Little Town of Bethlehem' (verses 1 and 2, tune Forest Green arranged SA).
14	Tableau: Mary and Joseph in the stable dejected. Other members of group slow down activities to depict night — sway to music if desired.		Spiritual: 'Kumbaya' (SA arr.) v. 1 Someone's crying . . . v. 2 Someone's grieving . . . v. 3 Someone's lonesome . . . v. 4 Someone's sleeping . . .
15	Shepherds in the field — rustic talk, etc. Others in group exit, except Mary and Joseph (on one side).		Anthem: 'Shalom' (SSA composed for the occasion).
16	Mime of fear, etc., and words like 'Listen! What's that?'		'Shalom' continues softly.
17	Mime of fear continues.	Angelic Speech: 'Be not afraid; for behold, I bring you good news of a great joy which will come to all the people; for to you is born this day in the city of David a Saviour who is Christ the Lord. And this will be	

	Action / Mime	Text	Music
18	Mime of fear continues.	a sign for you: you will find the babe wrapped in swaddling clothes and lying in a manger.' (St Luke 2:10–12 RSV.)	Last bars of 'Shalom' with crescendo and diminuendo.
19	Mime of fear continues.	'Glory to God in the highest and on earth peace to men of good will.' (St Luke 2:14 RSV.)	
20	Mime of fear continues.		Anthem: 'Rejoice!' (SSA composed for the occasion).
21	Shepherds exit to find the stable.		Carol: 'Sing Lullaby' (one verse SA arr.).
22	Mary, Joseph with doll or imaginary baby – mime.		
23	Mary, Joseph (with baby), mime.	Extract from 'Frost at Midnight' by Coleridge – 'Dear babe ... he shall mould thy spirit and by giving make it ask!'	
24	Solo dance: Interpretation of song – indicates death to come.		Solo song: Folk Carol – 'I wonder as I wander'.
25	Shepherds arrive at the stable. 'This must be the place.'		
26			'Yea Lord we Greet Thee' (v. 4 of 'Adeste Fideles' – 3 pt. arr. SSA).

SHORT PERIOD OF DARKNESS AND SILENCE

Item	Drama	Narr.	Choir
27	Procession of the wise men (from back of hall). (Lights blue.)		'In the Bleak Midwinter' – G. Holst (Carol) (verses 1 and 4, SA arr.).
28	Mime of journey by three wise men.	'Journey of the Magi' – T. S. Eliot 'A cold coming we had of it . . . I should be glad of another death!'	
		SHORT PERIOD OF DARKNESS AND SILENCE	
29	Group portrays secular aspects of Christmas.		
30	Group freezes: At each stroke of tambourine (Narr.) each member of the group makes one sharp movement towards the floor – last stroke leaves all lying on the floor.	Tambourine: 'Does the babe in the manger mean nothing to you?' Tamb.	Sp. 6 'Has the love, care and compassion He showed in His life-time for all men escaped you?'
		Tamb.	Sp. 7 'Have you forgotten "the man for others", born to die for you?'
		Tamb.	Sp. 8 'Look beyond the stable to the empty tomb of the Easter garden and accept the gift of New Life from the Risen Lord.'
			Choir: 'In Him was life, and the life was the light of men; He came unto His own and His own received him not.' (St John 1:4 and 11 RSV adapt.).
			Sp. 8 (loud) 'In Him, the Light of men, was Life; Choir (soft echo): 'was Life;
	All lie quite still.		

			Sp. 8 (loud): 'His own rejected Him,' Choir (echo): 'rejected Him,' Sp. 8 (loud): 'And there shall be no peace;' Choir (echo): 'no peace;' Sp. 8 (loud): 'If men are NOT of good will.' Choir (echo): 'If men are NOT of good will.'
31	Group rises slowly, as each member hears the Narrator. Group sits listening attentively, as if understanding for the first time.	Comes down from the stage.	'Christmas' – John Betjeman (last three verses). 'And is it true? . . . And lives today in Bread and Wine.'

SHORT PERIOD OF DARKNESS AND SILENCE

32	All exeunt (to back of the hall) dancing.	Exits with drama group.	Carol: 'Ding Dong Merrily on High' (all three verses SA arr.).

An extra feature we have not mentioned before should be noted, namely, the use of lighting effects and periods of darkness and silence. Furthermore, because most of the drama was improvised 'straight' mime or spontaneous activity with spoken words, the one solo dance that was included, performed by the director and accompanied by a solo song, proved particularly effective, with the light here playing a very significant part.

Although this production was a 'performance' in a sense, its character was not that of 'theatre'. The stage of the institute was not used, except that the narrator took up her position on one side of it, so that her words would be heard over the heads of the drama group. Staging blocks were used in the body of the hall itself, so that the players were raised a little. The choir was in the hall too, but behind the audience. There was then a sense that participants and members of the audience were all involved in the same experience.

Finally, because on many occasions different artistic activities took place at the same time, the sequence is set out in three appropriate columns – Drama, Narrator, and Choir.

Concluding Note

The above sequence shows clearly how through artistic media religious and challenging statements, in this case particularly in the solo and choral speaking sections, can fairly be made. The view of many members of the audience, from both performances given, was that the production made them think, yet in no sense did they feel they were under evangelical pressure. In the light of our earlier discussion in chapter 1, it is worth noting, moreover, that, though there were, of course, some participants who were members of various churches, others were agnostics or had no allegiance to a church, and yet were quite happy to play their part without feeling they were betraying their beliefs or lack of them. The sequence was certainly not a church production, but a village activity.

(9) **Festivals of Light**

Three of the major religions of the world each observe an autumn festival where light is the dominant motif. The overthrow of evil and the emergence of God are portrayed through this powerful symbol.

This sequence has three separate sections where Hinduism, Judaism and Christianity successively announce and explore their particular emphases, three groups of children being required altogether. It is suggested that at the end of each section the children involved should then withdraw as a group to one corner of the hall so that when three separate areas are thus occupied the final movement can take place. In this final action there is no attempt to merge the many lights although they each approach the others, for this would damage the separateness of each religion. Whilst we may compare and contrast this pattern with one where one prayer or action from a particular religion might be acceptable as voicing the beliefs of all, here the strength of the lights can be seen as the integrity of each of Hinduism, Judaism and Christianity is preserved.

(a) Hinduism: Festival of Divali

Some recorded Indian sitar music is played to evoke an appropriate atmosphere following which a dance-mime interpreting the myth of Rama's battle with Ravana is enacted whilst the story is read. There is a useful brief account of this dragon-slaying myth in P. Bridger's *A Hindu Family in Britain*, REP, 1969 (pp. 34–35). When goodness triumphs over evil this climax is marked by the lighting of two candles.

(b) Judaism: Feast of Chanukah

Separate reading from I Maccabees 1:20–24 and I Maccabees 4:36–51, 59 tell the story of the desecration of the Jerusalem Temple by Antiochus Epiphanes in 168 B.C., and its subsequent rededication after the victory gained by forces led by Judas of the Maccabees. A dance-mime illustrates this reading, stress being given not merely to the military exploits but also to the feelings of the Jews at the sacrilege enacted at the Temple and then their joy at its restored use for worship. As the reading finishes a recording of the triumphal march from G. F. Handel's *Judas Maccabeus* is played, in the closing stages of which are lit eight candles representing the Chanukah Lamp.

(c) Christianity: Christmas

This section opens with the chorus 'Break forth O beauteous heavenly light' from J. S. Bach's *Christmas Oratorio*. Then, accompanied by readings from St Matthew 2:1–10, St John 1:1–5, and St Matthew 5:14–16 a dance-mime explores the theme of the coming of Jesus as light to overthrow darkness and the challenge to His followers to be light to the world. The climax of this scene is the lighting of four Advent candles.

(d) Conclusion

Finally the three groups of participants come with their lights from their respective corners towards the centre of the hall. Here they form an outward-facing triangle, the candles being in front of the children. The final assertion can be spoken by all: 'God is light, and in Him is no darkness at all'.

(10) **Man's Destiny**

This sequence contains brief but characteristic examples of the aim of human life as seen in various religions. No attempt is made to synthesise these beliefs. They are placed together in sequence merely to permit an exploration of their salient features and to state concisely what is believed about God and the true end of man by different faiths.

(a) Music: Sitar-music – a recording.

(b) Reading: From 'Discourses of Jalal al-Din Rumi' (Sufi mystic). 'Though the roads are various the goal is one. Do you not see that there are many roads to the Ka'aba? For some the road is from Syria, for some from China. The variety is great and the divergence infinite; but when you consider the goal they are all of one accord and one. The hearts of all are at one upon the Ka'aba. Once they have arrived there it is realised that all their warfare and divergence was concerning the roads only, and that their goal was one.'

(c) Dance-mime: A group explores the contrast between man searching for salvation through material goals and worldly living, and man reaching his goal released from material concerns.

(d) Reading: From 'The Bhagavad Gita' (Hindu). 'But those who cast off all their works on Me, solely intent on Me, and meditate on Me in spiritual exercise, leaving no room for others, and so really do Me service, These I will lift up on high out of the ocean of recurring death, and that right soon for their thoughts are fixed on Me. On Me alone let thy mind dwell, stir up thy soul to enter Me; Thenceforth in very truth in Me thou'lt find thy home.'

(e) Music: The group will sing the chant, 'Hare Krishna'.

(f) Reading: St John 14:1–7 (Christian).

(g) Music: The hymn, 'I heard the voice of Jesus say, Come unto me.'

(h) Choral Reading: Psalm 27 (Hebrew).

(i) Dance-mime: This will illustrate the disobedience of the Israelites, using the prophetic writings. Thus, from Amos, the group will act out various social injustices, Amos' announcement of God's salvation if the people repent, and the failure to receive that gift resulting in conquest and exile (see pp. 115–118 below).

(j) Reading: The Qur'an, sura XXV. Choral reading of vv. 1–6, one person to read vv. 61–76 whilst the others act it. The title of this sura, *al-Furqan*, means 'The Criterion' and is applied to the Qur'an as the means provided to enable man to distinguish right from wrong (Muslim).

(k) Music: The *Nunc Dimittis* as sung in a Church of England Evensong – a recording.

Section Two
Learning from the Experiences of Others (introducing world religions)

Chapter 3
The Route

Since we cannot provide genuine personal experiences for all that must be taught, we now turn to the question of learning from the experiences of others, particularly in terms of considering the nature of religion itself and of introducing the world's major living religions in the classroom. We shall see that it is not simply a matter of British children being taught the facts of other faiths in addition to being given information on Christianity, even when they learn much from their immigrant classmates, nor is it just a matter of teaching the brotherhood of man and respect for different viewpoints and beliefs. We are concerned with an approach which attempts to explore the religious dimension of the universe as a unity, however that phenomenon has manifested itself to the different peoples of the world in the various periods of man's history, which, at the same time, though providing a 'common ground' of understanding, also does justice to the particular contributions of each religion.

We should therefore look at the ways in which a faith has been communicated through the various vehicles of expression so that the children acquire in the process some knowledge of the beliefs of that faith and understand something of the nature of the religious phenomenon itself.

If, for instance, we were to look at the Old Testament in terms of its providing and describing the expressions of the experiences of the adherents of a living religion at the time of its composition, we would, simply through examining the literary forms and word-pictures, together with the descriptions of ritual and worship, discover the 'message' of the Old Testament, without having to make a systematic study of Old Testament theology or doctrine, even if this could properly be done.

For example, we learn what Isaiah of Jerusalem understood by the 'Holiness' of God – the might, dominion, majesty, power, and glory of God – not because he tells us in so many words or discusses the theology of the concept, but because we read his verbal description of the vision of God's holiness in chapter 6, and, with artistic eyes, share in this vision. Isaiah himself apprehended this truth through a vivid experience while worshipping in the Temple. The seraphim embroidered on the awning above the altar seemed to become alive; the incense swirling upwards became the clouds of heaven; and the psalm being sung became the heavenly music of the hymn of glory – the Sanctus. The knowledge of God revealed through the experience could only be shared by a description of the experience. As we have implied, the theological insight gained, the method of communication, and the experience itself were all inseparably bound up with one another, and this gives us the clue for successful religious education today.

Thus, it should be clear that when we consider the questions of the material for religious education, the methods appropriate for communicating that material, and the insights to be gained – our aims and specific objectives for the topic or theme in hand – all these questions should be considered as one, all being inseparable aspects of the same process of exploration into the religious dimension of life.

It will also be clear from what we have said concerning the expressions of experience afforded by the literature of the ancient Hebrews that there is a basis provided by the Old Testament for studying living world religions. This can take place, not through the study of a supposed development of belief in Hebrew thought and drawing parallels with other religions,[1] but, because the Hebrew's experiences and methods of communication were natural to religion and appropriate for understanding the religious phenomenon, we can approach world religions through the same route by examining the significance of sacred places, the use of festivals and ritual acts, and expressions through the arts. This will also mean that we can begin to look at world religions at a much earlier stage than the 'parallel' approach would imply. For such a process, being concerned with beliefs and doctrines, concepts as concepts would have to be done within a course of secondary education during the adolescent period, whereas something of the approach advocated here can be done from the earliest school years. In any case, the bulk of learning from the experiences of others by this route is most appropriately done within the 8–13 age range, though the process would rightly be continued through the secondary period at greater depth.

In choosing topics or projects the following categories or areas of study will be helpful: sacred sites and buildings, festivals, rites of passage, customs and ceremonies, pilgrimages, pioneers or teachers, holy books, and stories.[2]

Bearing in mind the problems of time allotted to religious education on the timetable, and the danger of superficiality, we should not set out 'to do' each religion for each theme. We can look at more than one religion within a scheme, but should not attempt to compare too many. It is better to provide an opportunity of looking at a topic or theme in as much depth as possible for the age range concerned.

Moreover, for some of the categories, we must be careful to choose the most appropriate religions. For example, if we wish to look at holy books, we could choose Judaism, Islam, or Christianity, but we would avoid Hinduism, the Hindu literature being of less or even of no importance to the 'average' Hindu as compared with the regard for the sacred books shown by the adherents of those other faiths, though we have seen that we can use extracts from Hindu literature in the sequences of artistic experiences approach.

Similarly, if we want to look at Pioneers, we could study the life and experiences of the Buddha and gain considerably in our understanding of Buddhism as a whole and Hinayana Buddhism in particular. We could also examine the life story of Muhammad as a route into understanding the Islamic faith, provided, however, we make it clear that in no sense did he regard himself as the founder of Islam, and is not so regarded by Muslims. In other words, in Islam there is no parallel to the Buddhist's veneration of the Buddha.

The topic work will be brought more alive, of course, if we can find some way of enabling our pupils to participate and can give an air of informality to the lessons. Sometimes, actual objects of other faiths can be handled, like the Hindu figurines or the Sikh slippers we mentioned earlier,[3] while on other occasions the children can make similar objects for themselves, such as a garland as used in a Sikh wedding, or musical instruments, or very young children can dress up.[2] In addition, visits, properly prepared, to churches, synagogues, mosques and temples are, of course, most valuable and visits from religious leaders, clergymen, rabbis, imams and so on to talk about their faiths are very desirable if at all possible, provided we ensure that they know precisely what is required and expected from them.

We must also beware of assuming that all the beliefs found in a particular religion will be held in every area where that religion is embraced, or that ritual actions or other practices have the same significance for every adherent of a particular faith. Just as there are denominational differences in Christianity in respect of beliefs and practices and emphases of beliefs and practices, we should expect similar differences to arise in other faiths.

A classic example is afforded by the Hindu Divali festival. In some areas the festival of light is interpreted in terms of the goddess of prosperity or fertility visiting those homes where lights are burning and bestowing prosperity for the new year, particularly in respect of growth of crops. In other places, the festival is seen in terms of the world-wide 'dragon-slaying' motif, light overcoming darkness.

Moreover, whereas in general the same mode of expressing experience can be found in all religions, namely, through ritual and the arts, we do find, of course, that some art forms have not found favour in some religions, or in some periods of a religion's history. Thus, for example, in Christianity, with its history of colourful liturgies, music, drama, and literary expressions, we find nevertheless the avoidance, indeed, the rejection, of the dance form, because the early fathers, basing their views on their understanding of the use of dance in what they called the pagan religions, assumed that the dance was always suggestive of sexual licence, while the later Puritans feared that the dance engendered demonic magic. Only in churches founded through missionary work in a later period of history in countries with other religious traditions and customs firmly established was the dance form incorporated into the 'new' religion, as in the case of the African churches, and among the negroes enslaved in America and the West Indies whose worship, albeit transformed and given a new significance, retained the natural characteristics of African worship. We can then learn not only from the expressions that have been or are employed, but also gain insights into beliefs and attitudes from the lack of certain art forms or particular expressions within those forms in any faith, and particularly from the avoidance of a form by most adherents of a faith compared with the use of such a form in the same religion by others.

Finally, we can sum up the route advocated in this chapter by suggesting that one or two world religion schemes might be tackled in a way that in itself shows what we are really doing when we seek to learn from the experiences of others even in the ways described in terms of the 'shorter' topics and themes.

Choosing a particular religion and a particular place sacred to it (Jerusalem, for example, is important for Judaism, Islam, and Christianity, while the River Ganges is sacred both to the Hindu and the Buddhist), we try to discover why the place is held as sacred, see what buildings have been (or are being) erected, if applicable, and what the architectural design of those buildings tell us about the religion. Then we look at the paintings, the sculptures, the murals, the mosaics, the embroidery, and the furnishings, for all these again can reveal something of the beliefs and practices of the faith concerned. The schemes conclude by seeing what goes on in the buildings or at the sacred place in terms of rituals, festivities, dances, music, and so on – and why.

An example of such a procedure is given in the following chapter,[4] but in conclusion it should be observed that what we are trying to do in all the schemes within this approach, especially for the children from the strictly indigenous population, is to look at the world's major living religions in terms of the ordinary adherents of the faiths. That is, we are attempting, however imperfectly, and though the experiences are second or third-hand, to appreciate something of these great religions by putting ourselves in the position of those adherents, if but for a moment, in order that we might understand both the people and their religions better and with greater sympathy.

Notes

1. The older view concerning the so-called development of beliefs about God was re-expressed by R. J. Goldman in *Readiness for Religion*, Routledge and Kegan Paul, 1965, p. 179, though he allows for some regressions of thought on p. 178. He also sees in the study of such a development a course in comparative religions, i.e. of the Old Testament period. He does not go on, in fact, to see in this a parallel approach for looking at world religions as a whole, but it would be a possible line of approach, on the face of it, for any who wished to apply his procedure in this way, particularly if they were convinced by the parallel he does make between the intellectual development of the child and the progression of thought, as he sees it, in the Old Testament, and assumed that such a progression can also be found in the major living religions. It is another matter whether it can, and our whole approach in this book makes it clear that we would dispute the validity of an approach for religious education based primarily on the intellectual development of the child. In any case, in respect of the Old Testament the weight of modern scholarship insists that the position is much more complex and a simple developmental theory, even allowing for some regressions, must be abandoned. See on this: W. F. Albright, *From the Stone Age to Christianity*, 2nd edition, Johns Hopkins, 1946, p. 206; E. Jacob, *Theology of the Old Testament*, Hodder and Stoughton, 1958 (Fr. edit. 1955), pp. 65–67; H. H. Rowley, *The Faith of Israel*, SCM Press cheap edition, 1961, pp. 51 and 71–73 (1st edit. 1956); Th. C. Vriezen, *An Outline of Old Testament Theology*, Basil Blackwell, 1958 (Dutch edit. 1949), pp. 23ff., 30, and 175–180.
2. For many points and examples in this section I am indebted to a talk given by Mr Peter Woodward, Inspector Birmingham L.E.A.
3. See pp. 7 and 16 note 2 above.
4. No. 8 *The Sacred Ganges*, pp. 80–82 below.

Chapter 4
Examples
The Rev. A. L. Poulton and N. J. Lemon

Just as the examples in chapter 2 were designed simply to illustrate the Sequences of Artistic Experiences Approach, so similarly the schemes of work given here are offered as examples which illustrate the principles suggested in chapter 3. We shall therefore be concerned with the selection of some suitable themes and topics, the content for the schemes, and the order and arrangement of the material chosen. We have tried to provide as much information as is necessary for non-specialist teachers in particular to be able to begin undertaking work in what, for many, will be an unfamiliar area of study in their religious education programmes. At the same time we hope they will learn by teaching, without having to engage in a great deal of private study and reading, when, as is so often the case, time is limited or resources are not immediately to hand.

Consequently, we have restricted our suggestions for children's activities to examples of the kind of work that can be done by the children for the schemes as a whole or for certain sections, providing what seems to us the most appropriate and helpful exercises in these cases. Devising supplementary tasks for these sections, and similar work for others, is more properly the prerogative of the teacher, who knows his class and the children's capabilities and problems.

Finally, there is inevitably some repetition of material in the schemes. Educationally, however, this is valuable in terms of the general principle of reinforcement. In terms of the children gaining insights into the nature of religion and the particular religions discussed, such repetition is useful because it provides the opportunity for looking at some of the most important aspects and practices of the various religions from different view-points and thereby gaining a fuller and more comprehensive understanding.

(1) Sacred Meals

The two schemes under the heading 'Sacred Meals' illustrate the use which can be made of the theme with younger children (8 to 10s), under the title 'Eating Together', and with older children (10 to 13s), under the title 'Meals to Remember'.

(a) Eating Together (8–10)

(i) The People We Eat With

A   *People Who Call at Our Homes*

Under this title the children can write down a list of those who call: tradespeople, postmen, relatives, friends, etc. A master-list can then be compiled on the blackboard, and individual lists extended from it. The children are then asked to indicate on the list those who might be invited in for a cup of tea or an ice-cream, or even for a meal. A class bar-graph could be made showing the number of homes into which each type of caller would be asked; perhaps even the rent-man is welcome in at least one home! The point is made that we eat with our friends.

B   *People We Often Eat With*

Another list may be made under this title. The children are asked to list names of people they eat with rather than vague categories; for example, the children they sit next to at lunch-time, and the particular relatives who eat with the family regularly.

C   *People Jesus Ate With*

In a short discussion, obtain suggestions about the people Jesus ate with. This helps to 'earth' the children's ideas of Jesus, but will also begin to extend their appreciation of the significance of an action which Jesus himself used to express fellowship. As the list is built up (Joseph and Mary, the guests at the Wedding at Cana, the five thousand, etc.), the simple fact emerges that Jesus had a lot of friends. Some people thought he had too many! (St Luke 15:2).

(ii) The Value of Hospitality

Meals are particularly valuable to help people feel 'at home'. Mealtimes, especially after the day's work and at week-ends, can be seen as family occasions. Friends who eat with us become members of the family for the time being.

A   *Making our Friends at Home*

Discuss relevant courtesies: offering food before taking one's own; seeing that a friend is not left with an empty plate or cup; talking and listening. This right use of meals may be illustrated by its opposite: sulking, or refusing to eat, destroys the family spirit; being sent from the table may be a corresponding disgrace. Meals taken in silence (perhaps as a punishment, at school?) are quite different from social meals.

B   *Eastern Hospitality*

Reference may also be made to Eastern hospitality, by which the offering of a meal, even to a stranger if necessary, has always been looked upon as a sacred duty. The strength of this custom is derived from the nomadic background of some

Middle-Eastern peoples. A man who had occasion to take a journey away from his tribe relied on the welcome he would be offered by strangers he met on the way. There were no hotels in the desert! As he was at the mercy of his hosts, it was a point of honour to offer him the best hospitality befitting his rank, and to afford him complete protection during his stay. A man's generosity was often measured by the depth of ashes under his fire, for this showed how often he was prepared to share his food with others. Eating together was therefore the symbol of trust between friends; hence the horror of the psalmist's exclamation in Psalm 41:9, echoed in the gospel incident of Judas at the Last Supper (St John 13:21–30).

C The Raggedy Elf

The story is told of a miserly elf who lived by himself, disliked and unvisited. He hears of a 'best-kept house' competition in the village, with a bag of gold as a prize, and he works hard to win it. On the day of the contest he welcomes the judges, providing lavish refreshments for them and entertainment for the villagers. He wins the contest, but suddenly realises how empty his house will be when everyone has gone home. He sees the error of his ways, turns over a new leaf, and is never at a loss for friends from that day.

D A Special Meal

The children can write an account of a special meal (e.g. a party given by the Raggedy Elf after his change of heart), describing who was invited, what they ate, and what they did afterwards, to reinforce the lesson that eating together increases friendliness, as well as being a token of it.

(iii) Eating and Belonging Together

In this section we explore times when eating together is specially important. Local customs, such as the Harvest Supper, can provide additional material within the experience of the class.

A Birthday Parties

A review of the children's work on 'A Special Meal' in the last section will provide most of the elements for a picture of a typical birthday party. Additional distinctive features may now be noted, however:

1. gifts brought by the guests;
2. the singing of 'Happy Birthday to You'; and
3. the birthday cake. This is of particular significance, as it has the 'owner's' name on it but is not eaten by him alone, but shared; in fact the guests are supposed to 'leave room' for a piece, however small, as a mark of friendship.

These features all point to the same lesson: that we 'belong together' at a birthday party because we are all happy for the person whose birthday it is.

B Wedding Receptions

These have even more positive associations with the theme of 'belonging', as they bring together the families of the bride and bridegroom, often for the first time.

Children will be eager to share any recent experiences they have had of such occasions, particularly any girls who have come into their own as bridesmaids.

Customs vary widely, and it is easy to lose the thread at this point; but the following features can be shown to be common to all:

1. The bride and groom at the centre of everything, belonging to each other as never before. This is symbolized at a Jewish wedding by the couple sharing together the cups of wine over which the nuptial Benedictions have been pronounced. In this way they show their resolve to share whatever life has in store for them.
2. The reuniting of old friends and relatives at the meal table. Some will have come from a distance, and will not meet again until the next wedding in the family.
3. The cutting of the wedding cake by the bridal pair, who thus share their joy with everyone present.

C   *Christmas Dinners*

The children can be invited to write down where they had their last Christmas dinner and who shared it with them; members of the family, and probably other relatives or close friends. Against the names they could then note where everyone came from. A list of places on the blackboard, drawn from these notes, might quickly demonstrate that people are prepared to travel a long way at Christmas in order to be somewhere they belong.

The plight of the lonely and the elderly who have nowhere to go serves to underline the basic idea of belonging.

D   *The Jewish Sabbath*

In the home of the orthodox Jew, every week brings a day of special meals. The Sabbath, from sun-down on Friday to sundown on Saturday, is welcomed as a bride, so there is a touch of the wedding reception, especially at the first meal. The house is specially prepared, the best table-linen used, and the Sabbath candlesticks are polished until they sparkle – often a job for the oldest son. Visitors are particularly welcome, for the joy of Sabbath is a joy to be shared; and just as mother is ready to light the candles, she may enquire whether the children have grumbled their last grumbles and shed their last tears before Sabbath begins.

When the men return from the synagogue, where evening prayers have been said, all is ready. Two loaves are set at the head of the table, commemorating the double portion of manna gathered on the sixth day by the Israelites in the wilderness over three thousand years ago (Exod. 16:22). They are plaited to symbolize a bridal wreath, in honour of the Sabbath bride. Father, as the priest of the family, takes a cup of wine and recites prayers of blessing over it, recalling the six days of creation and the day of rest. The wine and the bread are shared by all present, and the solemnity of the moment quickly passes over into the warmth and gaiety of the ensuing meal, which has been looked forward to for the whole of a working week.

The noonday Sabbath meal is as eagerly anticipated, if young Jewish appetites can be judged by Gentile ones, for breakfast is not eaten before the long synagogue services of Saturday morning. A third meal is to be fitted in before dusk, so it is small wonder that the smells and tastes of the meal-table should impress themselves permanently on the mind of the Jew as he reflects on the meaning of the Sabbath.

The last moments of the day bring reminders of the everlasting Sabbath, which God will keep with His people in the holy warmth of the Messianic banquet at the end of time.

E *Sharing each other's Happiness*
The central theme may be recalled by the children drawing a wedding or birthday cake, with the words 'When we eat together, we share each other's happiness' inscribed around it.

(iv) The Cost of Eating Together
Eating together in the meaningful ways we have been exploring does not just happen; it must be planned for, worked at, and can sometimes be expensive. It is all the more valuable as a symbol for this reason. A number of different routes can be adopted to reach this moral.

A *The Cost of Food*
The price of a Sunday dinner can be made the subject of an associated arithmetic lesson. The people through whose work the food is brought to our table can be reviewed in geography. The labour involved in preparing and serving food is the concern of domestic science.

The real value of food can also be put in perspective by examining the condition of less privileged people of our own and other ages. It is precisely because the need for food is so basic to our natures that eating together gains the importance it has.

B *Very Special Food*
Some food has a value we cannot estimate. The story of David and the water of Bethlehem may be used to illustrate this (2 Sam. 23:13–17). Consider, too, the parents who go hungry so that their children may have enough to eat. This can lead on to a simple re-telling of the story of the Last Supper, in which Jesus showed His disciples that He was giving His life for them. The disciples could not understand this at the time, nor can we expect the children to grasp more than the simplest picture; but Jesus's careful planning of this last meal and His solemn words and actions showed how much He and His friends belonged to each other.

C *Gratitude*
The most fitting way to show our appreciation of our food is to eat and enjoy it. This is a parable for the whole of life, with all the good things God has given us to enjoy. The habit of gratitude, cultivated in response to the mundane things our scheme has been concerned with, is an essential element in the religious response to life.

The scheme can thus appropriately conclude with the children composing a poem or prayer of thanks for food, or a grace to be used at meals.

(b) Meals to Remember (10–13)

(i) Meals as a Symbol of Fellowship

The general considerations underlying the theme 'Eating Together' can briefly be drawn out in discussion. The value of asking a friend home to tea, and similar acts of hospitality, can be recognized more easily as the child grows older; likewise the importance of the host making the guest feel completely 'at home'.

A Biblical Illustrations

Considerable use can now be made of the Bible to illuminate the theme. For example:

Genesis 18:1–5: The story of Abraham and the angelic messengers illustrates the duties of Eastern hospitality, particularly in those regions where little refreshment would be available otherwise. Note that Abraham was not expecting the visitors, nor did he think they had business with him; yet he extended his invitation with great cordiality, and expressed it a privilege to do so.

1 Kings 17:8–16: The miracle to stress here is the widow's willingness to share her last morsel of food with the stranger! Had she not done so, she and her son would have died alone. In recognizing the need of another, she was saved.

John 6:1–13: We have two miracles here, the feeding of the five thousand, and the hungry lad surrendering his lunch! Some scholars have suggested that this example prompted others to reveal their own hidden stores, and the true nature of the miracle was in the new spirit which thus animated the hungry crowd as each man fed his neighbour. A parallel can be seen in the anecdote of the man who visited Hell, to find the inhabitants surrounded with magnificent food, but issued with spoons too long for them to feed themselves with. He then went to Heaven, to find precisely the same situation, though with one difference: all the inhabitants were busy feeding each other with the long spoons!

Luke 24:28–31: The Emmaus pilgrims were under no particular obligation to supply the stranger with a meal, but had they omitted the duty of hospitality, they would have lost the blessing. Older children may be able to say with little prompting how it was that Jesus was recognized as He broke the bread.

The Biblical principle, expressed in Hebrews 13:2, is clear from these examples: Remember to show hospitality. There are some who, by so doing, have entertained angels without knowing it. The practice of the early church referred to in Acts 2:46–47 is also illuminating.

B Feasts of Islam

Many other religious communities lay a similar stress on the sacred obligation of hospitality. Islam, as we would expect from its emphasis on brotherhood, has not overlooked the unifying nature of feasts, and two are given particular prominence.

The month-long fast of Ramadan, which calls forth a notable amount of staying-power (especially when it falls in the summer) ends naturally with a joyful feast, the 'Id al-Fitr, or 'Little Feast'. The return of the new moon is the signal for the donning of new or cleaned clothes, and the men engage in special services in the mosque. All the social delights of our Christmas are engaged in, and food is distributed to the poor, so that all may rejoice together. Even the dead are not overlooked, and pious visits are made to the cemeteries, to show that the ideal of brotherhood is not shaken by death.

The 'Great Feast', *'Id al-Kabir*, is primarily a commemorative feast, looking back to Abraham's 'sacrifice' of his son (cf. p. 63). As it is connected with the pilgrimage to Mecca, however, it is also a potent symbol of brotherhood. On pilgrimage all men are equals, and they all wear the same simple garments as they approach the holy city. As they eat together of the sacrificial sheep, this identity as brothers is emphasised. When celebrated at home, *'Id al-Kabir* provides another opportunity for sharing a meal with neighbours, and ensuring that the poorest of the community has enough to eat.

C   *Sikh Worship*

Food plays a prominent part in the service of the Sikh temples, where it seems to have been introduced deliberately to stress the equality of the worshippers and their fellowship with each other. In the order of service the *Granth* (the Sikh scriptures) takes pride of place, its ceremonial opening marking the start of worship. After prayers, expositions and singing, a passage is read and then the communion food (*karah parshad*) is distributed to all, without distinction of class or creed. Appropriately it is sweet to the taste, being compounded of butter, sugar and flour, and the service draws to a close as its sweetness is shared.

Brighter children may be able to find other examples of the symbolic use of food, whether in a secular or a sacred setting. For others, some of the material lends itself to presentation in drama or mime. We note elsewhere that the return of the prodigal is particularly suitable for this.

(ii) Meals and their Misuse: Breaking Fellowship

Material in this section may seem negative, but may be useful to consolidate the lesson of the last section by contrast with opposite lines of conduct.

As meals are seen as an effective symbol of fellowship, we may distinguish at least two ways in which the symbol can be destroyed: by refusal to enter into the spirit of the meal (or eating with bad grace); and by eating in the 'enemy camp', and thus lending support to the opposition.

A   *Eating with Bad Grace*

St Matthew 22 supplies two examples of this attitude: both the refusal of the invitation on inadequate grounds, and the refusal on the part of one to come 'properly dressed' (a currently fashionable form of protest!), shows that these people were not prepared to enter into the spirit of the occasion. Pharisees, too were condemned for seeking places of honour at feasts (St Matthew 23:6), as this showed contempt for other guests; the right attitude is enjoined in St Luke 14:7–11. The verses which follow specify that we should be ready to eat with everyone, not just our own select friends or with the spiritual elite, though Jesus was strongly criticized for this in St Matthew 9:10–13 and elsewhere. Further, the point of the story of Simon the Pharisee (St Luke 7:36–50) is that although Simon was prepared to invite Jesus to a meal (perhaps as an act of patronage), he omitted the common courtesies which the outcast woman was willing to offer.

Such attitudes were inexcusable in ordinary circumstances; but Paul's strictures in 1 Corinthians cs. 10 and 11 show that for him they were quite intolerable in the context of the love-feasts of the early church. These were expressly designed to demonstrate the fellowship of believers on the model of the Last Supper, and uncharitable behaviour at this point was shown up in its worst light.

The prime example is that of Judas, and the gospel writers emphasise this as a fulfilment of such scriptures as Psalm 41:9.

B   Eating with the Enemy

The same chapters of 1 Corinthians exemplify the second attitude, readiness to betray the fellowship by eating with the enemy. Remember that meat offered for sale in the market would normally have been ritualistically slaughtered, and so 'offered to idols'. Jews would be familiar with this idea from their own food laws, and its does show a more sympathetic attitude to the taking of life than our own callous destruction of livestock. However, the religious context raised an obvious issue of conscience for the scrupulous, and in Christian charity it was right for all to note this and act accordingly, so as not to cause offence. The language used in the discussion (see 11:14–21) is emphatic and worth close study.

For younger children, Daniel 1 makes a similar point more understandably; for if the young Jews had meekly accepted the king's food and infringed their own dietary laws in doing so, they would symbolically have shown their willingness to conform with the enemy in every respect.

The examples given above are all Biblical, but the theme is a basic one. Children should be encouraged to recall and write about further instances of betrayal within the setting of hospitality. Examples from Shakespeare include King Lear (betrayal by the family) and Macbeth, where the host himself is the traitor. History, English Literature and contemporary novels and films provide many examples.

(iii)   Special Meals

Special meals are often more rich in symbolism than appears at first sight. In bringing this out, it seems best to work from the more familiar meals, whose symbolic nature is of the simplest, to the less familiar but more richly meaningful examples.

Consideration has been given in the scheme 'Eating Together' of such familiar material as birthday parties, wedding receptions and Christmas dinners, which provide an obvious way in to the present study. The examples which follow have a common link in their commemorative nature.

A   Thanksgiving

The American Thanksgiving meal commemorates the coming of the Pilgrim Fathers and the founding of the nation. Americans thus 'return to their roots' at this time. They renew their sense of national pride by going back to a glorious moment in their history. Perhaps more significantly, however, they also individually place themselves within the nation's history at that point, even though their own ancestors probably arrived in America many years after the founding fathers.

B *The Jewish Passover*

A brief description of the Passover meal, the *Seder*, as celebrated in the Jewish home today, shows how deep-seated is this same sense of solidarity with their own people of all ages.

The *Seder* takes place on the first two nights of the Passover Festival, which is celebrated in the spring. The atmosphere of the occasion has already been suggested by the description of the Sabbath in the scheme 'Eating Together'. Special synagogue services mark the festival, but the significant action takes place in the home. This casts father again in his role as priest to the family, in direct line of descent from the patriarchs of Genesis. On the gaily decorated dinner-table, within his reach, are two objects which are vital links with the Hebrew slaves escaping from Egypt: the unleavened bread or cakes (*matzot*) enjoined in the Law, and a dish with a roasted lamb bone, the remaining token of the sacrificial lamb of Temple times. Other special foods bring to mind the anguish and joys of the Israelites in those early years when God was making them His own: a roasted egg, horse-radish and lettuce, parsley or cress, a saucer of salt water, a dish of mixed apples, nuts and raisins, and a large goblet of wine.

After prayer, the father kindles the lights and pours wine for all; he raises the seder-dish containing unleavened bread, and bids all who are hungry to share the festival. It is at this point that the youngest child has his moment of glory, putting the questions on the meaning of the festivities which he has rehearsed carefully beforehand, in common with countless generations of little boys before him (cf. Exod. 12:26–27). He is thus fully awake and aware as in answer he is told the thrilling story of the Exodus and God's redemption. Everyone present rises to the moment with prayers of blessing to God and the recital of the *Shema* (Deut. 6:4–5), the family prayer of Jewry. The ritual continues, including a hunt by the children for unleavened bread concealed about the room, with prayers and praises and the sharing of bread and wine, with the evening meal caught up naturally in the centre of it all.

The Passover begins as a kind of birthday party, because the Jew sees the time of the Exodus as the birth of his nation. It cannot end there, however, and like the Sabbath it concludes with psalms, hymns and popular folk-songs sung in hopeful anticipation of the coming of the Kingdom of God.

C *Holy Communion*

The same reliving of history is present in the Christian service of Holy Communion. Through it, the Christian sees himself as being present in the Upper Room by faith, as the Master symbolically gives himself to His disciples. The children should understand by now why Christ should have chosen the setting of this last meal for His final instruction of His friends, however much of the instruction itself may still be beyond them. All the symbolism we have considered above should add some small meaning for them to the Christian Eucharist.

(iv) Meals as a Symbol of Man's Partnership with God

A   *All Good Gifts* . . .

It is a religious truism that our food comes to us as a result of God's initial provision supported by man's co-operative effort; in these days of pre-packaged and synthetic foods, however, man's part has been increasingly emphasized; and no longer in the Western world are there many empty stomachs to stress the need for God to play His part! Good though this is, it has added to the materialism of the age; and the children should certainly be made aware of the fact that the comfortable situation of the developed countries is not shared by half the world.

The object-lesson of the manna in the wilderness (Exod. 16) is not without its humour, as one considers the plight of those who refused to obey the rules, and who woke either to the smell of putrifying manna on week-days, or to an empty larder on the Sabbath. The reception of each day's supply of goodness in grateful obedience was never an easy lesson to learn. For all the naive simplicity of the narrative, Jesus used it as one illustration of His own person and work (John 6:48–51). This should be studied in the context of the feeding of the five thousand earlier in the chapter. The Biblical incidents must be linked with present-day harvests if they are not to appear as isolated examples of magic.

B   *Social Application*

Man's partnership with God is often traced from the farmer to the transporter, the retailer and the cook, and younger children learn a lot from this about the functioning of society. The older child should be ready to go more deeply into the attendant problems of poverty, whether within the bounds of an affluent society (old age pensioners, etc.) or overseas. On which side of the man/God partnership in food supply has the breakdown occurred?

The work of local charities and such international relief organisations as Christian Aid and Oxfam could be investigated in some detail through their literature, and some schools may feel able to offer some practical help. Where appropriate, the work of religious communities could be examined as a history project, to show that 'social security' is no new thing.

Nor should the example of other faiths be ignored. For example the Sikhs, who give a religious value to food as we noted above, see its distribution to the poor as a constant religious duty. Every Sikh is expected to share his food with others, and to call for them when taking his meals. In addition, he is expected to support the system of the Free Kitchen (*guru ka langar*), a network of free hostels where Sikh and non-Sikh alike can receive food and hospitality for up to three days. In recent troubled years, the *guru ka langar* has provided a social service of incalculable value.

(2) Dress

The special dress of various religious traditions illustrates the understanding they have of God, and the personal attitude of the believer. The material in the scheme has been chosen to broaden the children's apreciation of the world's faiths.

The project will provide the opportunity for a liberal use of visual aids (film-strips, slides, posters etc.) and pictorial expression work by the children. Each child (or group of children) may produce a folder or booklet of work, and class friezes, collages, and posters may be made in addition at each stage of the scheme. Much of this pictorial work can be done with the aid of pictures taken from magazines, as well as by personal art work.

Of course, our principal concern is with religious material on our theme, but in this case it is particularly helpful to engage in some preliminary discussion in terms of dress in everyday life. Accordingly, the presentation is divided into two sections: (a) Preliminary Discussions and (b) The Religious Use of Dress.

(a) Preliminary Discussions

(i) Uniform and Formal Dress

We first consider the reasons for wearing uniforms:

A To show people belong together, e.g. soldiers on parade (especially in full ceremonial dress), footballers (where there must be no possibility of error in distinguishing who belongs to whom!), and school children, in schools where uniform is still used.

B To emphasize the function of the wearer, as is obvious in the examples already quoted. Further examples are nurses, firemen, policemen, clergy, nuns, etc. In some cases, the original reason for a particular uniform was purely functional, e.g. firemen's helmets, divers' wet suits, football gear. In other cases the choice is symbolic, and the symbolism involved may be discussed as these cases arise.

C To suppress individual quirks and weaknesses. School uniform was introduced to eliminate the obvious distinctions in dress between the children of richer and poorer parents. Soldiers must not 'do their own thing' but act as disciplined units within the army; their uniform is therefore impersonal, but is also used to define precise functions, by the addition of chevrons, red berets, best battle-dress or denim overalls, officers' batons or guards' 'cheese-cutter' hats.

A study of armour could be both useful and amusing at this point, as it illustrates how the utilitarian function can gradually be submerged in the desire for display. The knight could be well-protected, but if he fell off his horse he might not be able to remount without mechanical aid! The old-style red-coat of the infantryman looked very dashing as he marched off to war, but provided the enemy with an excellent target when he got there.

Children could make their own studies of particular types of uniform, finding out how they originated (e.g. indication of mourning for the death of Nelson in the Navy's uniform); some of the different forms they take (e.g. uses of different colours and styles to show rank in the uniform of nurses); and their usefulness for the job for which they are worn (e.g. firemen and policemen).

(ii) Informal Dress

The type of dress we adopt indicates how we want others to know us. The man who always appears in uniform wants to be considered at all times in connection with his function, not as a private person. The man who goes to the other extreme, of informality, is pleading to be accepted for what he is in his own person, without any reference to status in society. Most of us are inside the two extremes, as children will appreciate if they are asked to list the kind of clothes they wear in different situations, e.g. going to school, visiting relatives, going on holiday, or when left to their own devices.

Even informal dress is sometimes chosen with extreme care, and such apparently informal wear as that of the pop stars has actually become a uniform, to conform with points made in section (i).

At times we are conscious of being judged by the clothes we wear, e.g. a child in a school concert; a young man meeting his future in-laws for the first time; or a person being interviewed for a job. We may also be saying things about ourselves all the time without realizing it. The flamboyant extrovert dresses all the time to attract attention; the shy person keeps rigidly to orthodox dress for fear of standing out in a crowd. Often dress will reveal how far we think of ourselves as important in our own right, or as important by virtue of what we do. In the family circle most of us can afford to indicate that we are important in our own right; outside of it most of us betray less certainty!

Pupils can be asked to consider statues or portraits of famous men and women, or local notables. These appear in varied garb, in Greek or Roman robes, academic, legal, ecclesiastical or (more rarely) informal dress. They should consider why the form of dress was adopted for the 'sitting', and what it tells them of the nature of the person portrayed. Was he normally dressed like this? Young children have been known to be disappointed on meeting the Queen to find she is not wearing her crown, so portraits can be misleading on this point.

(iii) Symbolic Use of Dress

Though more obvious examples of formality have been eroded in contemporary society, we can still recognize specific instances of symbolism in dress, e.g.:

Rosettes, worn at football matches (in one's own crowd!); scarves, sported by members of the same school, college or football team; it is instructive to note when they are worn; wedding dresses, in white as a symbol of purity basically, though this can also be interpreted as freshness, associated with a new start in life; bridesmaids' dresses in assorted pastel shades, of more immediate interest to the younger girl; a sign that the attendants share in the bride's joy, and dress accordingly. The incident of the wedding garment in St Matthew 22:11–13, is apposite; presumably there was no practical reason why the guest should not have been properly dressed, but was merely refusing to join in the spirit of the occasion; hats, and their removal as a sign of respect when meeting people or entering church; 'widows' weeds', attenuated for the male to a black armband, where this is still worn, or a black tie; a means of advising people in advance that one is in mourning, so that the appropriate approach can be made; clerical dress, as a further piece of tacit advice as to the nature of the wearer.

As the collecting of pictures proceeds, children may like to indicate something of the symbolism in a word or two, e.g.:

Rosettes	Supporters
Scarves	Belonging
Black tie	Mourning
Clerical dress	Help available

Pupils should be in a good position by now to say what kind of uniform would be appropriate for each of the following, giving reasons briefly for their choice:

1. Electricity meter-reader
2. Funeral Director
3. Life Guard at the sea-side
4. Member of 'pop' fan-club
5. Bird watcher
6. Ship's captain
7. Ship's engineer
8. Monk
9. Engine driver
10. District Nurse

The artistic may like to go further, and design their own uniforms for each group.

(b) The Religious Use of Dress

(i) Judaism
The beauty of holiness was one ideal of the Jewish community in post-exilic times, and Ezra's work in beautifying both the Temple and the priests went a long way to restoring the faith of the Jews in Jerusalem, and their appreciation of the value of their traditions. Much of the material in the Pentateuch (or *Torah* – the first five books of the Bible), including the account of the priestly vestments in Exodus 39, is believed to have been overworked during that period. The end product shows a love of richness and devotion to detail which were used as an offering to God rather than as a means of personal display.

Today, Jewish men wear hats or skull caps when attending services at their synagogues, while the rabbi (who preaches, but does not conduct the service) is distinguished by his special hat. Wearing a hat at worship is for the Jew a mark of respect for God and holy things. (In similar fashion we may note here that the Muslim, who also claims to be a descendant of Abraham, removes his shoes as a mark of respect as he enters the mosque (cf. Exod. 3:5).) At morning prayers and festivals Jewish men also wear the *tallit*, a cloth of white silk or wool with blue or black stripes at the ends, and fringes (cf. Num. 15:37ff).

(ii) Christianity
The beauty of holiness tradition has often been followed by the Christian Churches, especially after the conversion of the Emperor Constantine. Elaborate sets of vestments are owned by many churches, not to magnify the importance of the wearer, but to indicate the value of his office.

Many other churches show a reaction to this, when the costliness of these elaborate displays has seemed to represent a social scandal. Thus some Christian societies, notably the Quakers, show by their dress and way of worship their desire to return to the ideal of absolute simplicity.

Even within these extremes, however, we may note the former trend: religious dress tends to be stylized in the manner of a uniform rather than everyday dress, because it is not the individual priest or minister who is of importance in his own right, but the function he performs within the religious community.

By way of showing the symbolic use of dress in Christian worship a list such as the following could be drawn up and initially the children could make their own suggestions as to the possible significance of each item: bishop's pastoral staves or crooks; the long black cassock – basic humility of the wearer; white surplice – purity or righteousness the minister must be prepared to don; the scarf or stole – the 'yoke' of Christ; the preaching bands – the evangelistic function of the minister; the plain dress in churches which stress equality before God rather than specialist function.

Denominational differences should not stand in the way of fruitful discussion, as the pupils attempt to explore below surface appearances to the basic attitudes and beliefs exemplified. Similar discussions can take place for the examples given below for other faiths, and reasons hazarded even when precise explanations are lacking.

(iii) Hinduism

A study of India is most useful in any attempt to understand the impact of religion on forms of dress.

The wearing of clothes and jewels of a deceased man by the *maha-brahmin* (an inferior rank of Hindu Brahmins) when he presides over the funeral rites, is based on the belief that this will provide the deceased with these belongings in the next world.

The official dress for formal occasions in India consists of a long coat with buttoned-up collar, and tight trousers called *churidar pajamas*, while professional people in the cities sometimes wear an adaptation of western clothes, jacket, trousers, and shirt. Head-dress indicates the rank, status, caste and place of origin of the wearer.

Caste, the traditional division of Indian people into four main groups signifying social status, occupation and religious standing, is shown by marks on the forehead, arms or chest. These marks, the *tilaka* or mole, may be in red, derived from red lead, in yellow, from sandalwood paste, or in white, from ash. Originally they were ownership marks, to show membership of tribal and religious groups.

Hindu devotees who regard themselves as the property of a god go further than this in identifying their allegiance, and may mark their foreheads with shapes and symbols known as Sect Marks, in the form of oblongs, triangles, circles, perpendicular lines, and so on.

A boy performs the Sacred Thread ceremony with his father to confirm that he is a member of his caste, if he belongs to one of the three highest, or twice-born, castes. At worship a Hindu is stripped to the waist and his feet are bare. He wears the sacred thread over his left shoulder and across his body to the waist.

(iv) Sikhism

Sikhs are immediately recognizable by their beards and turbans. More precisely, however, there are five items of dress (in a general sense) which signify their religious allegiance and devotion – the 'five Ks':

Kesh (uncut hair) – marks the Sikh's devotion to God;
Kanga (comb) – is worn in the hair to symbolize religious discipline;
Kachs (shorts) – stresses religious freedom, as they originated in the need for physical freedom and movement in battle;
Kara (steel bracelet) – encircles the right wrist and denotes strength and unity; and
Kirpan (sword) – symbolizes authority and justice.

The wearing of the turban is an additional mark, as it shows the willingness of the Sikh to be immediately identifiable amongst members of other faiths. The importance attached to this has been illustrated in England over the refusal of Sikhs to conform to regulations enjoining the use of crash helmets, and their request to retain the turban even when wearing the uniform of bus conductors.

(v) Buddhism

Buddhist monks are distinguished in five ways:

Saffron-coloured robes and an alms-bowl which symbolize the monk's dedicated religious life;
a strainer which enables him to save the life of any minute creature contained in his drinking water;
a razor for shaving the head each *uposattha* day (the days of the full and new moon);
a needle to mend his robes; and
beads to assist him in meditation.

These are the only personal objects the members of the *Sangha* (the Buddhist order of monks) are entitled to own.

(3) **High Days and Holidays**

(a) Holidays in History

We tend to think in personal terms of holidays, as each family makes its own plans for the use of leisure; so it may be necessary to build up the children's awareness of the social nature of holidays if they are to feel their way into the historical material. There are conflicting forces at work here: shift work, diversity of occupations and the mobility of the population, which tend to break the social pattern; and school holidays, the week-end habit, youth camps, holiday camps and the surviving practice of 'Wakes Weeks' and large-scale industrial holidays serving to strengthen and perpetuate it. Socially, few of us feel a holiday to have been a real holiday unless others have shared it with us. The holiday agencies and colour supplements can provide the teacher with an abundance of material to make this basic point.

As far back as we can go, people have taken the chance to 'down tools' and enjoy themselves from time to time. This hasn't just been a negative reaction to work, however! They have always found a good reason for the habit in some special event. In some parts of the world a birth, a marriage or even a death can be the occasion for a family or village to stop work for days. This would seem to be an admirable way to show that there are more important things in life than daily work and making money.

Most holidays, however, have been commemorative of some event in the past. The Christian festivals are the most familiar examples, though immigrant children may be able to give others. These fostered the sense of solidarity (or simply of belonging) within Christendom, and the customs accompanying the holidays emphasized this.

There was a feeling, too, that the great men of the past still belonged to the people, and for this reason the Saints' Days were celebrated with enthusiasm. This habit seems to have snow-balled in mediaeval times, to the extent that normal work became difficult in view of the great number of holidays. Children should be able to work out for themselves the effect of this in an agricultural community before mechanization.

With the Reformation, very many such observances were swept away, and only St Valentine, along with the national patron saints, receives much popular attention today. It is worth recalling some of the more colourful customs and the home-spun lessons to be gained from them, however, and a number of good source-books (including children's encyclopaedias) are available to provide information. Historical novels frequently give graphic accounts of the way holidays were spent, and the customs of May Day, Hallowe'en and St Nicholas (the day the boy bishops were created) need little imaginative embroidery to hold the attention. This is a rich field for discovery, however, and the brighter children will be able to find out much for themselves.

As they begin this scheme, it is valuable for pupils to make their own broad approach to the subject. If the following short questionnaire is used, some time could be given to class discussion of individual answers to question 1; an element of competition could be induced by drawing up exhaustive lists for questions 2 and 3; and inventiveness could well range throughout the social, sporting, farming and television calendars in answer to question 4.

1. Give three good reasons why people have holidays.
2. What special holidays did people have in the past?
3. What special holidays do we have today?
4. Invent a special holiday, and say how you think it could be observed.

(b) Holidays in the Bible

The sacred festivals of the Jews exhibited all the characteristics we have been considering. Joy was of their essence; they were social occasions, when it was no less than a religious duty to participate; and in their theological interpretation they brought the people back to their basic convictions about God and their relationship to Him.

(i) The Passover

Originally thought to be a pastoral festival, when the first-fruits of the flock were offered to God in sacrifice, in historical times the Passover had been firmly re-interpreted as a commemoration of the deliverance from Egypt. Though it is described as one of the occasions when the people should 'appear before the Lord' (i.e. in the sanctuary), the most characteristic part of the festival was observed in the home. Here, by symbolic act and formula, the Jewish family placed itself dramatically with the earliest families as they fled from Egypt, saved by God Himself. Feasting, play-acting and love for the oft-repeated ritual must all have combined in their power to mould the developing minds of the children, and to confirm the adults in their faith. This was a holiday which would be enjoyed all the more as a conscious participation in the freedom which God had secured for His people.

(ii) Pentecost

The reaping-season, which began at Passover, ended 50 days later (after a week of weeks, 49 days) with Pentecost. A less elaborate festival than the Passover, lasting only one day, Pentecost was used to commemorate the events associated with Mount Sinai, the giving of the Law (Exod. 20) and the establishment of the Covenant between God and His people (Exod. 24). To the Jews, the Law was not something to be resented as an imposition, but to be accepted with pleasure, as a sign of how they could live as God's people; it became 'the bright jewel in the Jewish crown', and its bestowal was the occasion for joy. We gather this, too, from Nehemiah 8:9–12, on the occasion of Ezra's publishing of the Law to the people of post-exilic Jerusalem.

Thus alongside the usual gaiety of harvest, which children often need reminding of when they are too acclimatized to tinned food and deep-freezes, came the sober consideration of the privileges and responsibilities of God's people.

(iii) The Feast of Tabernacles

Held in the autumn, this was a full week's holiday, and linked with the final in-gathering of the produce of the land: corn, wine and oil. Traditionally the people lived in temporary huts for the week, as they might have done during the busy days of harvest, but their time was spent in religious rites and social enjoyment. The situation had such obvious affinities with the days of the wilderness wanderings (at least as seen through the comfortable mists of time) that it is not surprising to find this festival being used to commemorate that period of national history. Those were the early days of salvation from Egyptian bondage, days of dependence upon the miraculous provision of God, days full of promise of the corn, wine and oil of the future when they would be in their own land: all the materials of the happiest holiday of them all.

Much of this material has verbal, visual and dramatic force. Groups of pupils could also work on one of the festivals, finding out how it was observed in Biblical times or today in Israel or among Jewish communities elsewhere. Each group could then present its findings.

(c) Going away on Holiday

Additional material for this section can be found in the scheme on 'Journeying with a Purpose' (pp. 61–64). If that scheme is to be used, this section could well be omitted from the present work. The following notes indicate only the obvious links with the foregoing, and a suggested method of approach.

(i) Jerusalem

Deuteronomy seems to have envisaged that all Jewish men would go to the central sanctuary for each of the three major festivals (12:5–7, etc.). Later, when Jerusalem became an increasingly important focal point for the devotion of the people, they would make their pilgrimage there as often as possible, even from a great distance, and especially at significant times in their lives. This is the background of Jesus' visit to the Temple at the age of twelve (Luke 2:41–50).

We can imagine the sociable nature of these expeditions, which varied little in essence until the time of Chaucer's *Canterbury Tales*; short extracts from Chaucer's Prologue might be of use in showing the children what a fourteenth-century pilgrim felt like. Much more to the point, however, the 'Songs of Ascents' sung by the Jews as they climbed on their way to the Holy City (Psalms 120 to 134, and especially 122) are evocative of the joy of the traveller in sight of his goal. These pilgrimages would be the ancient equivalent of holidays spent away from home. Children will readily appreciate the thrill of preparation and departure, the excitement of the city with its awesome Temple, and the quiet satisfaction of the homecoming.

(ii) Mecca

Pilgrimages to Mecca, dealt with in detail later, could be discussed at this point, to illustrate the fully-rounded nature of the pilgrimage experience in its three aspects:

1. Social. The crowds converging on Wembley for the Cup Final feel something of the sense of 'belonging' generated by the pilgrimage, but only a pale reflection of the full experience, lacking the religious motive and being divided by partisanship for the opposing teams! Pilgrims discover their unity at the end of the journey; and a million Muslims a year achieve this goal.

2. Religious. The Pilgrimage to Mecca is one of the basic duties enjoined on all Muslims. They go there out of obedience to Allah, not for their own enjoyment. They see themselves as part of the great brotherhood of Islam, and set aside their own interests as unimportant beside this.

3. Personal. One custom (not usually observed today) is for the Muslim who has completed his pilgrimage to dye his beard red. He will never be the same again, and everyone will know it.

(iii) Pilgrimages Today

A lot of travel agents, and a number of specialist tour operators, arrange modern pilgrimages of various sorts, e.g. to Lourdes, Rome and the Holy Land. Nearer home, the idea of the pilgrimage is returning. The writer remembers a party of young people meeting in their parish Church at eight o'clock on Easter Monday morning for Holy Communion, before they walked the fifteen miles to the shrine of St Alban, where thousands of other young pilgrims were gathering. On a slightly less exalted level, a Cheshire headmaster took a party from school on a pilgrimage to the tomb of the 'first man to be run over by a railway engine'; needless to say, the other treasures of Liverpool Cathedral were not overlooked that day.

Set the pupils to discover a suitable site for pilgrimage in the region. No parts of Britain are completely bereft of such interest, and a lot of local history can be absorbed in the process. If time can be found for a pilgrimage to be organized, keeping in view the social, religious and personal aspects studied above, so much the better.

(d) Christian Holidays

So much work is done in most schools each year on the themes of Christmas and Easter that it may not seem necessary to add a section here on the principal Christian festivals. In the present context, however, the holidays themselves can be examined from the children's own experience, to see how far they answer to the kind of holidays we have been considering. We must be prepared to accept such experience as it stands, though there is value in helping children to understand it at a deeper level.

(i) Christmas

This festival is a major experience in the life of nearly every child in Britain, in one way or another, so we do not meet with the problem of helping children to feel their way into it.

The most potent symbols of the holiday are those connected with giving, just as the first question they greet each other with when the great day has dawned is, 'What have you had for Christmas?' This is not a dubious manifestation of childish materialism, but in part a genuine delight in the fact that, for some strange reason, adults who normally think twice before giving anything away are all suddenly prompted by unwonted generosity. Linked with this is the habit of families to spend the day together, and the general air of kindliness and freedom from criticism which most people are able to maintain for the occasion.

These things are the raw material of the Christmas experience, of which the events which go on in Church or are spoken of in R.E. lessons are interpretations. We have to ask ourselves what is 'real' for the child, and it is a good rule of thumb to say that what goes on in the home is 'real' in this sense. We can then offer the Christmas story as a real reason for doing these real things. Beneath the symbolism lies the fact that God has revealed Himself within the love-relationship of a family.

He is there for all, just as the Christmas scene is displayed in the big stores as well as in Church. The symbols are pointers to this truth, which cannot be adequately presented in abstraction. The holiday can be more effective than a hundred text-books.

To explore Christmas from this angle, pupils could be asked to give the reasons for the following Christmas customs, and to say whether they help or hinder our understanding of the message of the season:

1. The giving of Christmas presents;
2. The arrival of Father Christmas at the local store;
3. The school Carol Service or Nativity Play;
4. Family visiting over the holiday;
5. The usual spectacular programmes on television;
6. The sending of greetings cards;
7. Christmas dinner;
8. The extended Christmas holiday.

For brighter pupils, a classroom debate could be staged between Scrooge and his clerk, Bob Cratchit, on the advantages and drawbacks of Christmas, on the basis of their sentiments set out by Dickens in *A Christmas Carol*:

Scrooge: What's Christmas time to you but a time for paying bills without money; a time for finding yourself a year older, but not an hour richer; a time for balancing your books and having every item in 'em through a round dozen of months presented dead against you. If I could work my will, every idiot who goes about with 'Merry Christmas' on his lips, should be boiled with his own pudding, and buried with a stake of holly through his heart.
Cratchit: Christmas is a good time; a kind, forgiving, charitable, pleasant time; the only one I know of, in the long calendar of the year, when men and women seem by one consent to open their shut-up hearts freely, and to think of people below them as if they really were fellow-passengers to the grave, and not another race of creatures bound on other journeys. And therefore, Uncle, though it has never put a scrap of gold or silver in my pocket, I believe that it has done me good, and will do me good; and I say, God bless it!

(ii) Easter

To help children capture the flavour of Easter, attenuated to a degree in contemporary Britain, full reference must be made to the long penitential season of Lent with its attendant privations, the increasing solemnity of Holy Week, accompanied by ritual enactments of the events of Christ's Passion, and the extreme austerity of Good Friday and its prolonged services of penitence. After all this, the lighting of the Paschal Candle at midnight on Holy Saturday in many Catholic Churches heralds the return of life to a weary world! The darkened Church is suddenly ablaze with light as the members of the congregation light their own candles from the central flame, and the colour and music of the great Easter services take over, with the message, 'Christ is risen!'

In Eastern churches, the Great Service of midnight is preceded by a procession outside the Church representing a search for the body of Jesus in the tomb, a custom of the Church of Jerusalem which has spread widely in the East. It was from a similar ritual re-enactment of the meeting of the women with the angels at the tomb that some scholars trace the origins of the great mediaeval cycles of Mystery Plays in England.

Beside such celebrations, the experience of the children may seem limited. Many of them will still accompany their parents to Church, however; the public media give prominence to the Easter story; and the first outdoor holiday of the year, with new life bursting through on all sides, still retains its attraction for each new generation.

While younger children may be encouraged to discover further Easter customs, and find out what eggs have to do with the feast, older children may be ready to discuss the evidence for the Resurrection. This is presented dramatically, in terms they can appreciate, in the novel by Frank Morison, *Who Moved the Stone?*; and as a play, by Ladislav Fodor, entitled *The Vigil*.

(4) Journeying with a Purpose

By studying what are obviously purposeful journeys we hope to help children towards an understanding of religious activities related to specific sites and particular people. We may not expect to take the children on such pilgrimages, but by using literary, visual and dramatic methods we may aim to make the children aware of what the pilgrim anticipates and receives to aid him in his understanding of the faith he professes and practices.

(a) Judaism

In the Hebrew Scriptures it is possible to see the pilgrimage practice and requirements current among the Jews until the destruction of Herod's Temple in A.D. 70. Deuteronomy 16:16 outlines the obligation of thrice-yearly visits to Jerusalem for the Pilgrim Festivals; *Pesach* or Passover (Exod. 12:21–27), *Shavuoth* or the Feast of Weeks (Lev. 23:15–22), and, *Succoth* or the Feast of Tabernacles (Lev. 23:34–43). This historical base to communal pilgrimage celebrations is of great importance to the Jews. Illustrations of later fulfilment of these commands are found in the single childhood episode of the life of Jesus when the journey to Jerusalem was the custom of many villagers from the north (St Luke 2:41–51), and the return to their homeland for Jews from many nations at the time of the Feast of Weeks (Acts 2:1–13).

The centrality of Jerusalem in Jewish worship followed from Josiah's reforms (2 Chron. 34). The Psalms, especially those usually known as the Songs of Ascents, show worshippers visualizing and approaching Jerusalem (Ps. 121), and then praising God in or near the Temple, perhaps singing with the priests in religious procession (Pss. 24; 122–4; 133–5). Thus there is added to the historical base an emphasis on one particular place where God is best approached and known.

Today the pious Jew, hoping to see evidence of the coming of the Messianic Age in the renewed use of the Holy City for religious purposes and revering the actual ground of the Holy Land, prays at the Wailing Wall of the Temple, kisses the ground as he arrives in Israel, and perhaps offers the traditional farewell, 'Next year in Jerusalem' in connection with the observance of Passover.

Sacred territory evokes special worship, rests on secure historical framework retelling the Acts of God among His people, and reaches forward to future expectations.

(b) Christianity

A visit to any Roman Catholic Church will afford the opportunity to see the site of a simulated pilgrimage in the form of the Stations of the Cross. Pictures or carvings describe the events of Jesus' final journey from Pilate's house to the entombment, fourteen separate incidents being noted. In Holy Week congregations visit these stations arranged on the interior walls of churches, whilst at other times of the year this devotional exercise may be followed by individuals, sometimes on an open hillside site in the form of a Calvary. Early pilgrims to Jerusalem followed such a traditional route and this local pattern permits worshippers to make a similar journey, saying prayers and meditating in order to identify themselves with the sufferings of Jesus.

Pilgrimage to the Holy Land itself has known many forms and as many motives. The restoration of 'Christian' control over the places associated with the life and death of Jesus suggests a belief in the necessity of access to the material site of the Incarnation, and if this is so then the military aspects of the medieval Crusades are means to the end of lay participation in the surroundings in which Jesus lived and worked. The modern traveller to Israel and Jordan may not be a pilgrim overtly, in the sense that his journeys will not involve specific ritual and devotion, but in experiencing someone talking from a boat on Galilee, seeing a synagogue ruin at Capernaum and noticing the sort of village Nazareth is he will be able to appreciate the setting in which Jesus delivered his sermons and parables. The background information of the Gospel setting becomes as important as following the prescribed pattern of religious activity.

The Pilgrim's Way leading to Canterbury illustrates the journey undertaken in the belief that the places where saintly people have worked and died are themselves worthy of contemplation and reverence, and that prayers offered there are especially effective. After Thomas Becket's death in the cathedral, the intention of all who travelled to Canterbury, whether by Chaucer's direct route from London or on the ancient North Downs trackway now romantically called the Pilgrim's Way, was 'the holy blisful martyr for to seke'. This encounter might be at the spot where he died, at his tomb or through various personal effects displayed for veneration. Shrines, such places having relics of Christian saints, enabled people living in material surroundings to appreciate the person and work of these saints through their own material associations. St Thomas' shrine at Canterbury is paralleled by examples at Durham (St Cuthbert), Westminster (St Edward the Confessor), Chester (St Werburgh) and St Alban's among others.

(c) Islam

'Pilgrimage to the House (i.e. the Ka'aba in Mecca) is a duty people owe to God, for those who can afford the journey.' This Qur'anic injunction illustrates the religious journey which is an obligation rather than a meritorious optional element in one's religious life. Any description of the *hajj*, the Greater Pilgrimage, will note a complete unity of action absent in many other pilgrimages. It takes place at a set time of the year, all pilgrims wear simple identical clothing, all observe the same ritual in or near Mecca at the same time. They sacrifice all personal identity and status alongside fellow Muslims from many different cultures and backgrounds. But even the *'Id-al-Adha*, the joyful Feast of Sacrifice which marks the close of the pilgrimage and is celebrated across the Muslim world, is not merely a statement of unity and brotherhood. The whole intention of pilgrimage and its associated feasts is Islam, the creation of the spirit of submission to the Will of God, and as such this act is the highest form of devotion that the Muslim can give for it symbolizes his complete self-offering to God. The historical picture which stands behind the believer's willingness to sacrifice everything is that of Ibrahim's (Abraham's) intended offering of his son Isma'ail (Ishmael).

(d) Buddhism

Although Buddhism's doctrines do not involve supernatural beings or a divine creator, its stress on sacred journeys is one example of activity indistinguishable from religious actions.

Four great centres of pilgrimage between them describe the life and progress of Gautama Buddha. Thus the Buddha's followers visit Lumbini in Nepal where he was born, Bodh Gaya in the Indian state of Bihar where he attained enlightenment, the Deer Park at Banaras where his first sermon was preached, and Kusinara where he passed into *pari-nirvana*. This following of the Buddha's path is an attempt to understand with him the problem of suffering in the world, and the physical pilgrimage which the Buddhist undertakes is a picture of the inner pilgrimage in quest of enlightenment. Since the actual journeys are obviously impossible for the majority, extensive use of iconography permits simulated pilgrimages within the confines of the temple or indeed the home, the various postures of the Buddha images evoking appropriate forms of meditation.

Additionally, relics of the Buddha are venerated in many countries in the East. In Sri Lanka are the Temple of the Tooth at Kandy and a tree grown from a cutting taken from the original Bo-Tree. Burmese pagodas possess hairs from the Buddha whilst his footprints may be found in Japan. An identifiable background connected with material remains and places where truth has been pronounced form a solid foundation for the Buddhist's meditation, an essential stage on the road to wisdom.

These few examples, which have not even included anything of Hindu, Sikh or Japanese origin, should not be taken as a comprehensive picture but merely as pointing towards certain features and principles. The diverse reasons for pilgrimage afford children the opportunity to build up different pictures, in written, visual and map form, of the places, events and people concerned and to discover any central aspect at each site and shrine. By compiling diaries of the journeys involved in bringing Muslims together for the *hajj* at Mecca, or calendars outlining the observances and festivals of the Old Testament or modern Jew, children can be introduced to a breadth of discovery and experiences which both set the pilgrimage against a world backcloth and localize the event in the expectation of the pilgrim. Any such collection of project work, both describing and interpreting the actions of believers, is indeed a book of world religions.

(5) Sacred Buildings

This scheme aims to show how the design and arrangement of places of worship say something definite about the beliefs of the people worshipping there and about the nature of God as approached and experienced in those forms of worship. Architecture, plan, adornment and furnishings are themselves seen to speak of the relationship between man and the divine: alternatively it may be the absence of works of art or the position of the building within a wider environment which makes the most salient point about the beliefs of any religious community.

Ideally the child should be able to enter the church, mosque, synagogue or other building: there he may sit, look, absorb and touch within appropriate limitations according to the beliefs and feelings of those who worship there. Realistically the teacher will need to help the children simulate the experience to be gained within the building.

(a) Christianity

(i) Anglican and Roman Catholic Churches

Starting with churches most likely to be found near any school, we seek features of considerable prominence which stress basic beliefs and attitudes. To this end the children should be encouraged to note what strikes them most forcibly.

Externally, the church or cathedral may be seen to be set on a hill, particularly if its foundation dates back many centuries: this is a symbol of the hill of Calvary or of a martyr's death, e.g. St Alban's Abbey. Another dominant feature seen before actually entering the church will be a tower or spire, proclaiming the centrality of the Resurrection. A development in symbolism is found where three spires have existed, or are still extant in the surviving example at Lichfield: later generations than that of the builder could employ this picture to teach about the Trinity. Again, the Kingship of Christ over His followers is depicted in the lantern tower of the Roman Catholic Metropolitan Cathedral in Liverpool.

Internally, the traditional cruciform shape complements the symbolism of the spire: here is the Cross, the other central historical fact of Christianity. From the West Door children can attempt to sense the importance of worship at the altar in such churches. Architectural devices are employed to stress the worshipper's approach to God whether in the progressive narrowing from nave through the choir to the sanctuary or by steps which separate these different sections. Walls, steps and aisles seem to proclaim that the altar at the ecclesiastical east end of the church is the focus of all attention: here is the spot where the Eucharist, the central act of worship in these traditions, is celebrated.

The other fundamental symbol within the building is the placing of the font, where Baptism is administered, near the main entrance door: through baptism the recipient enters not the building but the community of the Christian Church. Other points to be noted by the children will be the arrangement of the seating, denoting the respective functions of congregation, choir, servers and clergy; and the position of the people within the nave stresses the security of Christians in the *navis* (Latin) or ship, this being analogous to the Ark in which Noah's family was saved.

(ii) Free Churches

In such chapels or churches the initial object should be to discover that the apparent absence of much decorative furnishing is as significant as its presence. Again there is a need to discover any focal point of attention: traditionally this has been the Pulpit. Here the Bible may be seen displayed. It is read, and an exposition of its meaning is given in the Sermon. The positions of the pulpit and the Bible together points to God confronting His people through His Word in every service.

The grouping of pulpit, font and communion-table speaks of the various actions and services associated with them taking place within the believing community and not at any distance from some worshippers. If decoration is employed it is likely to be verses from the Bible: God's Word, whether it is read, preached, or sung, is thought to be sufficient by itself to make people aware of His presence.

The prominence given to the Baptistry in a Baptist Church or among the Churches of Christ shows the emphasis placed on Believers' Baptism when entering the community.

(iii) Eastern Christianity

Slides, other pictures and diagrams may be necessary to help children visualize the interior of an Orthodox Church. With these aids there again emerge the central features which enable the Orthodox worshipper to commune with God.

The internal plan is of a Greek Cross, roughly square, whose central space is covered by a dome or series of domes. The space which lacks seating allows worshippers to mingle together, or to come and go during the service: such informality speaks of people being at home in God's house. Icons seem to fill the church, whether framed or as frescoes or mosaics: worshippers place lighted candles before the figures of Christ and the saints, which visible images are said to link the worshipping community in the church with those standing before God in heaven. Thus the building itself communicates a sense of timelessness.

The most important visual feature in front of the congregation is the Iconostasis, a solid screen which divides the sanctuary to its east from the lay congregation. An icon of Christ in Glory is above the screen whose central doors, the Holy Door or Royal Doors, open during the Liturgy to reveal the altar or throne and to permit the Little Entrance when the Book of the Gospels is brought out, and the Great Entrance which is a procession of the communion elements from the north chapel to the altar for consecration.

The Presence of Christ in the sacrament, the importance of the Eucharist symbolized by the Iconostasis and the ritual behind it, and the total community of Christians are all prefigured by elements of the building itself.

(b) Judaism

The interior of a Synagogue must be investigated to determine what beliefs can be described by its furnishings: it is to be noted that although this faith proscribes images and representations of God, there is still room for use of the arts to make religious assertions.

Prominent on the east wall is the recess where the Ark is kept: the Ark contains the *Sepher Torah*, the Scroll of the Law, and is the most sacred possession of a synagogue. Reverence for the Law is seen in the various coverings and adornments connected with the Scrolls: a mantle, crown and breast-plate together symbolize its stature. The Law is carried in procession from the Ark to the *bema*, or reading desk, in the centre of the synagogue: this central *bema* is where the Law is read and explained and from where prayers are offered. During prayers the congregation faces the east wall, marking the direction of Jerusalem.

The seating is seen to face inwards, the community of Israel being emphasized by this arrangement which allows no distinction between the different men of the congregation: the only restriction is that ten adult males form a *minyan*, the quorum needed for public worship in which the Law is read and prayers said.

Visual decoration is limited to writings from scripture which may be inscribed on the walls, often in the form of the tablets of the Ten Commandments. The Star of David and the *menorah*, an eight-branched candlestick used during the Festival of Chanukah, are also to be seen.

Together these various elements of the interior of a synagogue all lay stress on the Law as being the means whereby Judaism knows it has been chosen by God for His purposes and whereby believers can know God's presence among them. Among the daily Benedictions offered by Jews is: 'Blessed art Thou, O Lord our God, King of the Universe, who hast chosen us from all nations, and given us thy Torah.' The Law is absolutely fundamental, both in buildings and in prayers.

(c) Islam

The Mosque seems to be the simplest of buildings among places of worship: thus the children will have to discover beliefs expressed in the absence of furnishings. The minaret, an open court containing a fountain, and the *mihrab* or prayer-niche in the covered prayer hall may be the only immediately discernible features.

The fountain, or the taps similarly providing running water if the mosque is in a colder country, demonstrate the necessity of purifying oneself before approaching God in prayer. The *mihrab* marks the direction of that approach, for it is sited on the *qibla* wall which faces Mecca: since all mosques face Mecca, whether that direction is to the north or south for example, the Muslim world appears to be a gigantic wheel gyrating on Mecca as its hub. All worshippers are thus united in their prayers, following the Qur'anic command: 'From whatsoever place thou comest forth turn thy face towards the sacred mosque'.

The minaret, often graceful, seems dominant from outside: although it is used by the muezzin who stands at its top when calling the faithful to prayer five times daily, it does not actually feature during the worship itself. Similarly the *mimbar*, or pulpit, which stands to the right of the *mihrab* is not essential to the offering of prayer but is for the sermon which is delivered only on Friday at the time of the noon prayer.

Adornment of the walls of the mosque, both inside and out, is strictly non-representational, but it has an extremely positive point to make in that it always contains much calligraphy, the highest of the Muslim arts. The writing is of verses from the Holy Qur'an. Together with the *kursa 's-sura*, a lectern for the cantor who kneels facing the *qibla*, these inscriptions which face or surround the Muslim stress his central belief that God has revealed Himself to mankind through the Qur'an which was received by the Prophet Muhammad. The common actions of the whole Muslim community, united in prayer throughout the world, are in obedience to the commands contained in the Qur'an. Thus what seems to be a building lacking in many furnishings says through its apparent emptiness that God, who may not be depicted in any visual form, is to be followed with complete obedience.

The significance of sacred buildings can best be shown through filmstrips and slides together with the teacher's own observations in the fields of art and architecture and his appreciation of the different liturgies and rituals enacted within the various religious traditions, reinforced through artistic work appropriately undertaken by the children, such as model-making, and producing plan drawings and pictures that are impressionistic rather than full of detail.

Of course, where possible, visits to local places of worship of various religions will naturally provide a fuller appreciation of patterns of activity experienced by one's closer neighbours. Thus we can help the children to see something of the broader vision of the whole human condition.

It is important also, however, that both through their own artistic work, and through any visits, the children acquire the necessary vocabulary regarding the buildings, words like church, chapel, cathedral, synagogue, mosque, gurdwara, and temple, providing the starting points. Similarly, the vocabulary related to the furnishings connected with worship in the buildings must be noted. The correct identification and description of altar, communion table, *bema*, and *mihrab*, for example, should lead to an appreciation of how Christians, Jews, and Muslims are able to express their beliefs through what they place in their buildings for worship as well as through the architecture of the buildings themselves.

The principles and methods of working outlined here, together with an almost limitless extension of an investigation of correct terms and collection of plans and pictures of different places of worship, are capable of being applied to the Christian denominations and other world faiths which have not been mentioned in this scheme.

(6) Talking with God

Prayer is one of the most basic human experiences. It is found in the earliest forms of religion of which we have any knowledge, and keeps a central position in the most highly developed. The different forms of prayer retain an amazing consistency throughout the whole range of human faiths. In spite of the intellectual arguments which are constantly being levelled against it, each new generation takes to it in its own way, and finds its own reasons for doing so.

The aim of this scheme is to look at ways in which men pray in a variety of religions, so that pupils may come to a greater apprehension of the nature of prayer. They will already have their own views formulated in a rough-and-ready or highly articulated way by their experience since early childhood. It would seem necessary for this reason to introduce the course with a discussion in which preliminary misunderstandings may be resolved, so that some measure of objectivity may be brought to the study.

(a) Clearing the Ground

(i) The nature of prayer should be discussed broadly, probably after pupils have been asked to spend a short time writing out their own views on what prayer is and what it achieves. The following definitions are typical of the variety of views prevalent, though often unexamined, in modern society:

A profitless exercise, designed to draw the mind away from solving present difficulties and working to overcome them, in the hope that God will intervene and solve them for you; a simple escape mechanism when life is becoming too involved.

A source of strength to an elite minority, most of whom lived a very long time ago, or indeed may be only legendary figures; if they did exist, they surrendered most of what makes life worth living for the sake of this power.

An attempt to twist the arm of the Powers that be in order to achieve one's own ends.

A complicated procedure, only successfully mastered by highly eccentric people who are probably mediums.

An unknown and insufficiently investigated force, which could be of incalculable benefit for the good of mankind if sufficient research was carried out into harnessing it.

A means of achieving a measure of serenity and protection from the buffetings of fate.

The means whereby you can enter into fellowship with God and do His will.

A way to show gratitude for the good things of life.

(ii) Several of these presuppositions will be reviewed in the course of the religious studies which follow, but one basic point should be drawn out of the discussion straight away, the distinction between religion and magic. The third alternative above, though expressed more roughly than many people would commit themselves to, shows a common attitude which owes more to magic than to religion. Basically, prayer requests 'Thy will be done', while magic demands 'my will be done'. Magic rites are an attempt to bind the spiritual forces for man's ends, while religion is the attempt to enter into relationship with them, or Him.

A test case may be proposed for discussion, a case which happens to be true:

The son of a devout church-woman was seriously ill, and she prayed fervently for his recovery. Against the odds he returned to full health and strength, but to her constant anguish later turned to dissolute ways, so that in the end she felt it might have been better had he not recovered. As she put it, 'I feel God is punishing me for demanding his recovery'.

Was the woman's reaction healthy? Was her explanation acceptable? Was there an element of magic in her idea of prayer? What attitude towards God did it foster?

Attempts have been made in the past to show that magic preceded religion in man's experience, so that prayer was a later development, but these have not been substantiated. This shows that the instinct to enter into a right relationship with God or the gods is at least as basic as any desire to manipulate the divine power. The two exist side-by-side to the present day, and pupils should be ready to distinguish elements of each in the phenomena they study.

(b) Judaism

(i) The Work of Prayer

For Jews prayer is a part of their work, done for God in accordance with His Law. They are left in no doubt on this point, for the duties of prayer are enjoined on them in the *Talmud*. So they tackle the work of prayer in the same spirit that they undertake their other duties. They do not expect to receive any great emotional or spiritual experience from it, but they see it as an important part of their daily offerings to God.

In the days of ancient Israel, the most significant form of prayer would not have been verbal at all; it would have been the sacrificial offering selected from flocks, herds or crops. Whatever words accompanied the ritual, it was this objective act which counted, for it was this that was enjoined in the Law. The satisfaction arising from a worthy sacrifice willingly offered was the most characteristic satisfaction afforded by Temple worship.

When the Temple was destroyed in 586 B.C. and the Jews were taken into exile, they took with them a law which prevented them offering animal sacrifices anywhere other than in Jerusalem (see Deuteronomy 12:5–7, etc.). Their desire to make their offering to God, however, was strengthened rather than diminished. So it came about that they accepted the full demands of the Law, as far as they could still be undertaken in an alien land, and in place of the sacrifice of animals or crops, learned to substitute the offering of prayer.

Eventually the synagogue replaced the Temple as the active centre of worship in Judaism, but the business-like approach to God was not lost in the process. Generalizations are dangerous in matters of religion, but we may say that the sense of prayer as a duty, albeit a freely accepted and often joyful one, has never been lost by the Jews. They do not ask what they have received from it, for prayer is not necessarily to be rewarded by mystical experience or physical benefits. They believe that pleasure in religion comes from giving rather than getting. Narrow forms of pietism, then, are foreign to the spirit of Judaism; so the Law lays it down that ten men are required as a quorum for the offering of public prayers in the synagogue; the work of prayer can then proceed at the hands of a properly constituted meeting.

(ii) Thankfulness

Another strong characteristic of Jewish prayer is that of thankfulness, and this needs to be brought into focus if pupils are not to gain the wrong picture from the foregoing stress on duty. Of all the nations of the world it would seem that the Jews have had the least to thank God for, and yet no race has devoted itself more energetically to giving God thanks. A brief reference to Jewish theology suffices to explain this. As Jews are sure that everything comes from the hands of their creator God, they are sure that no pleasure can come to them from any other source. Not only that; for they are as fully committed to a salvation theology as the Christian, though for them the Exodus probably represents the salvation event, through which they became children of God in a special way, which is represented in Christianity by the death and resurrection of Christ.

Thankfulness is the chief mark of the three times of prayer which the Jew observes daily, times which correspond to the times of the Temple sacrifices of olden days, in the morning, afternoon and evening (or night). The principal feature of each of these prayer-times is the *Tefillah* (prayer), now popularly called the *Amidah* (standing), for it is to be recited standing. It consists of eighteen benedictions, of which three at the start and three at the end are in praise of God and in thankfulness for his bounties. Secure in this setting of gratitude come the petitions for those things of which God's people have need.

In addition to grace before meals, the Jews offer thanks for a great variety of other benefits, such as the witnessing of some natural event like a rainbow (see Genesis 9:8–17) or a thunderstorm, meeting a great man, moving to a new home, or even enjoying the scent of a sweet herb. They extract the material of devotion from each passing moment.

(iii) The Great Debate

The central prayer of the Jews is not a prayer at all on most men's understanding of the word; it is rather an affirmation, known as the *Shema*: Hear, O Israel! The Lord is our God, the Lord is one (see Deuteronomy 6:4). It is as if the Jews are not speaking to God at all, but to themselves and their fellow Jews, constantly exhorting to faithfulness. This is not untypical of much of the contents of the Jewish prayer-book. One affirmation follows another, and all are to be accepted, even where they may seem to disagree. Yet life is like this, and Jews train themselves through prayer to accept it, not without question, but as the only pattern we have, and one that we must accept. Life is good; it comes from the hands of the loving creator; and yet we have to put up with a great deal which does not seem good to us under any circumstances. We can't solve the paradox, we simply have to live with it.

It is not surprising, then, that a sizeable amount of arguing with God goes on in Jewish prayer. Perhaps as the Jews did not choose to be God's people, they feel a greater freedom to argue if they feel hard done by! A good example of this outlook is the prayer of Rabbi Levi Yitzhok:

> Good morning to You, Almighty God,
> I, Levi Yitzhok, son of Sarah of Berditchev,
> Have come for a judgement against You,
> On behalf of Your People Israel.
> What do You want of Your people Israel?
> The slightest thing, and You say,
> 'Speak to the children of Israel'.

It has been suggested that this spirit of honest questioning helps to explain the custom of standing for prayer. The Jews feel at liberty to stand their ground before God, for they are commissioned to understand His will and truth, and a slight distance needs to be maintained if they are to approach these things objectively. Certainly the habit seems to be ingrained, for the Old Testament has several prime examples:

Genesis 18:22–33: Abraham argues with God over the fate of the cities of the plain.

Genesis 32:24–28: Jacob wrestles with the angel of the Lord to obtain a blessing. It was from this incident that he gained his new name Israel (perhaps 'one who wrestles with God'), which, all things considered, is an entirely appropriate name for the nation.

2 Samuel 12:15–23: David prays for the life of his child. This is an important example, for it shows a readiness to acquiesce in the will of God if the striving has not achieved the desired result.

Jeremiah 20:7–18: This is the most poignant of the confessions of Jeremiah, from which we get a vivid understanding of his spiritual struggles. Note how outrageously honest he is at the start, how he approaches a firmer faith, and how he relapses into a more vindictive spirit.

We may conclude that the duty of absolute honesty in prayer, even if we call God's activity into question, is one of the Jews' greatest insights.

(c) Christianity

It may not be necessary to deal with the Christian teaching on prayer very extensively at this point; firstly because this is probably the only teaching about prayer the pupils have already received; and secondly because Jesus, as a Jew, inherited and transmitted much characteristically Jewish teaching on the subject.

(i) The Jewish Heritage

On the Jewish heritage, we may note that Jesus formed his band of twelve men, who at any time could constitute a quorum for the purposes of prayer and worship. At the same time, we see them making a regular practice of attending worship in the Temple, a practice maintained in the earliest days of the Church (Acts 2:46, etc.). In condemning the Temple traders, Jesus made it clear that He saw the Temple as the proper setting for the prayers of God's people (St Matthew 21:13).

The marks of Jewish prayer noted in the previous section are also prominent here:

The New Testament is full of the spirit of thankfulness, derived from the Master Himself. Once the saving moment of His death and resurrection was passed, the Christians saw themselves as already set for the 'promised land', or the kingdom of God, precisely as the Jews had done after the Exodus, and this added to their sense of gratitude.

Jesus continued the great debate, and we do an injustice to His humanity if we fail to recognize this, and see Him merely as being on the end of a 'remote control' system operated by God! Thus He was in favour of importunate widows (St Luke 18:1–8, and cf. St Luke 11:8), who pestered the life out of their Judge until they got justice and refused to pretend things were all right when they weren't. However, he was bitterly opposed to those who pretended to pester God with their long prayers and self-justification when all the time these were empty words. The Gentiles are accused of this in St Matthew 6:7; and the Jews in the parable of the Pharisee and the Publican (St Luke 18:9–14). He continued His own discussions with God to the very end of His earthly life, in Gethsemane (St Matthew 26:39) and on the Cross itself (St Matthew 27:46), while showing the same absolute willing submission to the will of God as it became clear to Him. It was in His own fierce striving that He learned to teach His disciples, when they prayed, to say, 'Thy kingdom come, Thy will be done'; a prayer every Jew subscribes to fully.

(ii) Other Characteristics of Christian Prayer

Some things may seem special about Christian prayer, though we may not claim them as unique. I would simply note here the 'three Fs', though pupils in some schools may be willing to suggest others. The three Fs are:

Forgiveness

Because the Cross is central in Christian teaching, confession and the acceptance of forgiveness have taken a central place in Christian prayer. This is not a morbid exercise, as some maintain, for the prayer of Jesus at the Cross, 'Father, forgive them, for they know not what they do' (St Luke 23:34), shows that the most outrageous sins are open to forgiveness, and so are 'dealt with', and left behind. The secure knowledge of forgiveness brings its strength to Christian prayer.

Faith

Forgiveness brings with it the assurance that the believer is already a member of the family of God, and that his Father has his interests at heart (St Matthew 6:25–34). This faith enables his prayer to be outward-looking, to God and to His world.

Freedom

This background brings a characteristic freedom to the Christian which is widely misunderstood. He is free to choose, for example, the forms of prayer and worship which he finds of most benefit, rather than having certain forms prescribed. On the one hand, he may adopt a formal, highly-structured type of worship, conducted in elevated language which he carries with him into the personal place of prayer. On the other hand, he may choose the most informal and unstructured means of approach, typified most clearly in the plain and homely meeting-house of the Society of Friends (the Quakers). The danger of this situation is that he may see the choice as a purely personal one, and forgo the strength of commitment to a body of believers; but it does lay the stress on the primacy of inner conviction and reality, which cannot be by-passed by passive reception of church membership.

(d) Islam

The study of Islam has a strong attraction for those who are brought up in an atmosphere of hazy Christian liberalism, simply because it seems the most straightforward of religions. The five pillars provide a clear-cut prospectus for the believer: the Declaration of Faith (*shahadah*), Prayer (*salat*), Fasting (*sawm*), the Poor-due (*zakat*) and Pilgrimage (*hajj*). Their clearly-defined path contrasts with the complex guidance of the Jewish Law and the apparent uncertainties of the Christian law of Love. Prayer is central, and the manner of prayer is not left to chance.

(i) The Call to Prayer

Muslims pray five times daily. The prayer times are *fajr*, the dawn prayer (between dawn and sunrise); *dhur*, the early afternoon prayer (just after mid-day); *'asr*, the late afternoon prayer; *maghrib*, the evening prayer (just after sunset); *'isha* the night prayer ($1\frac{1}{2}$ hours after maghrib).

The call to prayer is traditionally given by the *muezzin* from the minaret outside the mosque, at each time of prayer. Fundamentally it is a call to submission, for the primary characteristic of Islam is submission to Allah. The call is in the following form:

God is Most Great, (repeated 4 times)
I bear witness that there is no deity but God (repeated twice)
Come to prayer, come to prayer,

Come to success, come to success,
God is Most Great, God is Most Great,
There is no deity but God.

The specified times of prayer, the call from the minaret, and the use of the mosque for communal prayer, especially at mid-day on Friday, all serve to underline the other chief characteristic of Islam, the brotherhood of all believers.

(ii) The Practice of Prayer

Precise regulations govern the practice of prayer for the Muslim. Before prayer, ritual ablution is prescribed, in running water if this is available; hence the fountain in the courtyard of mosques in Islamic lands. If no water is available the ritual can be adequately discharged by a form of dry cleansing, either with sand or by a simulated symbolic action. Adequate dress is prescribed during prayer, though the shoes are removed. Prayer may be performed almost anywhere, but the immediate area of prostration must be clean. For this reason the use of a prayer mat is normal though not obligatory, and the prayer mat is sometimes thought of as the Muslim's private mosque. The mosque is carpeted throughout for the same reason. Prayer is always directed towards Mecca. The niche in the prayer-hall of the mosque indicates the right direction for the worshippers there, and Muslims will take care to familiarize themselves with the direction in other places, by the compass if necessary. This direction is south-east 40 degrees in the United Kingdom.

The sequence of prayer is carefully observed. After an inward resolve, the worshipper raises both hands to the ears while standing, saying aloud *Allahu akbar*, God is Most Great. With hands on chest, he then recites the *Thana'*, an act of praise, with verses of the Qur'an. After a further *Allahu akbar*, with hands raised, he then bows down and repeats three times, 'Glory be to my Lord, the Great.' He stands again for the *Allahu akbar*, then prostrates himself twice with his forehead to the ground; between the prostrations he sits upright on his heels, saying again *Allahu akbar*, which is further repeated when he rises from the ground. Personal prayer may follow, but not until the formal requirements of prayer have been completed.

Even this brief description may serve to show the prominence of the doctrine of submission in Islam. The effect of the practice was expressed thus by the Prophet: O ye who believe! seek help with patient Perseverance and Prayer: for God is with those who patiently persevere.'

(e) Eastern religions

Short of a full-scale study, it is difficult to pass on sufficient information about Eastern religious thought to make any real sense to Western children. The theme of prayer cannot be adequately completed without some reference to Eastern thought, even at this simple level, however. The pupils need to be aware of other dimensions of thought on prayer, even where they may fail to appreciate them. The following brief notes are intended to serve to this end.

(i) Prayer in the Non-theistic Religions

Jainism, an Indian religion with 1,500,000 adherents, is noted for the great beauty of its worship and temples, but it has no doctrine of a supreme creator God. Logically prayer is excluded, especially as the life of the believer is seen to be controlled by *karma* (fate), but in fact prayers form part of the devotions, offered by the devout three times a day for 48 minutes each time. The aim of these devotions is the characteristically Eastern one of union with reality, which in spite of fate is to be actively sought for by the individual. 'The soul is the maker and the non-maker, and itself makes happiness and misery, is its own friend and its own foe, decides its own condition, good and evil.'

In these circumstances it is easier to think of Eastern prayer as meditation, though the wrapt contemplation of serene images of the *jinas* (saints) reminds one of the invocation of saints in Western religion. The *jinas*, however, are perfected and so are already indifferent to human affairs, and their contemplation is undertaken so that their spirit may be emulated, leading to the attitude of renunciation and preparation for Nirvana.

(ii) The Round of Prayer

Many examples may be quoted of practices based on the efficacy of repeated prayer. Prayer wheels may be found in Buddhist temples in Tibet and Nepal, giving rise to a background noise of bells attached to them, as the worshippers walk round the shrine in a clockwise direction, bearing candles and joss-sticks. Rosaries are in use in many religions, including the Parsis (traditional Persian religion) and Buddhists as well as Catholic Christians. Their use ensures the regular recitation of traditional formal prayers. Hindus make use of pictures, books, *yantras* (geo-metrical designs in wood or metal) and *mandalas* (designs in powder, executed in five colours) as foci of meditation. Their use of *mantras*, brief formulae repeated over and over again, is paralleled in the West with the use of the Jesus Prayer, 'Lord Jesus Christ, Son of God, have mercy on me', by members of the Orthodox Churches. These practices should not be dismissed unexamined as 'vain repetitions', for their thoughtful use is enjoined. It is said of the *Ahmavar*, the basic prayer of the Parsis, that one sincere repetition has as much value as a hundred *gathas* (hymns).

It can be recognized that the recital of prayers may be thought to generate its own power. Thus Chinese Buddhists make some use of intercessory prayers to the Buddha, for the welfare of the nation, perhaps, and for all living beings; but fulfilment of these prayers is looked for rather through the transfer of merit arising from the recitation of the prayers than from the intervention of the Buddha.

(iii) The Prayer of Union

In its most advanced forms, Eastern prayer is set to achieve a state of union with reality. Typically we think of this state in the form of the Buddhist Nirvana, seen either as escape from the imprisonment of this life by renouncing its pleasures, or more positively as the fruition of life with the unfolding of the Buddha-nature in the individual. It has been said that the ideal of Nirvana has become a substitute for the idea of God, suggestive of unsuspected links with western religion.

(f) The four faces of prayer

The most satisfactory way in which pupils can continue their own studies to consolidate this work is to explore one particular faith in greater depth. It will be of use to them in closing to analyse the experiences of prayer broadly, so that they can determine whether the 'fully-rounded' experience is present in the faith they study. A brief analysis may be of use to this end, based on the acrostic 'ACTS'.

(i) Adoration

It is the art of seeing the Universe and its Creator as something far greater and more important than small selfish interests. It enables the worshipper to see himself in God's world rather than looking for God as a useful addition to his own world, just as Copernicus saw the earth revolving round the sun instead of the sun and stars revolving around man's little earth. Above all, adoration provides man with an outlet for the sense of wonder and mystery without which his religion is dead and his life is colourless.

(ii) Confession

Far from being a morbid exercise, confession is entirely healthy, as long as it is linked with the idea of God's forgiveness and acceptance. It enables the worshipper to give up the game of pretence whereby he tries to appear better than he really is, and so to accept his real self and gain a proper self-respect. It may often enable the worshipper to deal with unresolved conflicts and fears because they have already been 'dealt with' by God.

(iii) Thanksgiving

This gives expression to the relationship of grateful dependence which is natural between a man and his Maker. It encourages a spirit of lively expectancy for the future, based on experiences of God's goodness in the past; and it strengthens the conviction that life is a matter of grace, to be enjoyed, rather than a dull round of duties to be performed in the hope of eventual reward.

(iv) Supplication

Often thought of as the only kind of prayer, supplication cannot stand by itself but must naturally flow from the foregoing. At its simplest, supplication seeks to bring the needs of man into relationship with the resources of God. Thus, it never instructs God what to do, but rests on the faith that He knows what is required and is willing to supply it.

Resources

Judaism
Isadore Epstein, *Judaism*, Pelican, 1959; Lionel Blue, *To Heaven with Scribes and*

Pharisees, Darton, Longman, and Todd, 1975; Rev. Dr A. Cohen, *Everyman's Talmud*, Dent and Dutton, 1932.

Christianity
Einar Molland, *Christendom*, Mowbrays, 1961; Igumen Chariton of Valamo, *The Art of Prayer* (tr. Kadloubovsky and Palmer), Faber and Faber, 1966.

Islam
Kenneth Cragg, *The Call of the Minaret*, OUP, 1956; *Islamic Correspondence Course*, Minaret House, 9 Leslie Park Road, Croydon, Surrey, CRO 6TN, 1973; *The Koran*, Everyman's Edition, J. M. Dent and Sons Ltd, 1909.

(7) Community and Communion

Most religious traditions have a place for the special identifiable community. These communities display varying emphases according to their purpose. In this scheme we hope, through studying the salient features of the concept and practice of community in a number of religions, to provide a view of the beliefs which emerge from this basic expression in religion. There is insufficient room to discuss every aspect of, for example, the *Khalsa* or the Church, but a more comprehensive picture can be established by cross reference to material in other schemes, notably those on Dress (pp. 50–55) and Journeying with a Purpose (pp. 61–64).

(a) Buddhism: the Sangha (or Samgha)

The Buddhist monk, as identified by his dress and possessions described elsewhere, belongs to a community founded by Gautama Buddha himself. If his vows are permanent he attains the position of the highest form of *bhikkhu* (almsman), but he may belong to the *Sangha* for only a pre-determined shorter period, as in Burma where most males receive part of their education in a monastery or for a few days when mourning a close relative or indeed for any length of time.

More prominent features of the *Sangha*, however, include its position in the credal statements of Buddhism. It is one of the Three Jewels of the faith and its existence is therefore a necessity as is stated frequently in the formula, 'I go to the Buddha for refuge, I go to the *Dharma* (the Buddha's Teaching) for refuge, I go to the *Sangha* for refuge'.

Whilst the monk obviously renounces the world, as is symbolized by his conforming to ascetic dress and behaviour and his acceptance of particularly rigid laws, he maintains a close relationship with the outside world. Monks and laity are interdependent, the laity gaining their knowledge and teaching through the monastery and the members of the *Sangha* receiving each morning their material support from lay Buddhists practising their charity by filling the monk's begging bowl.

Thus in the life of the Buddhist monk we see an essential but specialized community which nonetheless remains integral with the wider world of Buddhism.

(b) Sikhism: the Khalsa

The ascetic, celibate and monastic ideal finds no place within a Sikh schema. Fellowship is total, embracing all members of the faith and indeed those of other religions. Although we may again identify the Sikh by particular forms of dress, we must also explore other dominant aspects of his community life.

The *Khalsa* (Pure Ones) was established as a sacred brotherhood of men and women by the tenth Sikh Guru, Gobind Singh. Their special dress of the Five Ks and their new additional names of *Singh* (Lion) and *Kaur* (Princess) identified and identifies them to the point where they will risk loss of employment, imprisonment and even fighting in defence of their faith to maintain these essential binding traditions. There is no special priesthood, only a total Sikh community.

That community, however, is not exclusive. It abhors the traditional Indian pattern of caste division and insists that separation by religious grouping is also hateful. Sikhism's founder, Guru Nanak, taught that 'There is neither Hindu nor Muslim'. The Sikh communion meal, the *karah parshad*, uses a common bowl to unite all worshippers and participants, again denying Hindu caste restrictions and Muslim food regulations. Each *gurdwara* (Sikh Temple) today has its *guru ka langar* (Free Kitchen or Temple of Bread) where hospitality is given to all regardless of their background.

Entry into the community is deliberate at an age of discretion when new members undergo the initiation ceremony of *Amrit*. Here the identifiable community embraces all within the religion and points to its belief in One God and a united people.

(c) Islam: the Umma

Whilst Muslims are essentially those who can repeat the *shahada*, 'There is no Deity but Allah and Muhammad is his Messenger', truly practising believers are often defined as those 'who establish regular prayer (*salat*) and practise regular charity (*zakat*)' (Qur'an 4, 162). The *Dar al-Islam*, or House of Islam being an area where a total religious, political and legal Muslim practice is observed, already points to an essential difference between the western view of the separation of sacred from secular and the Muslim understanding of the *Umma* as an inclusive term embracing not only the people but the whole application of the faith as well.

The hours of prayer, the Ramadan Fast and the Pilgrimage to Mecca are referred to elsewhere. Here we may note the particular emphasis on the insistence that the community is not founded as a human institution. All such are merely transient for, 'To every community there is a term' (Qur'an 7, 34). Rather the *Umma* is the product of the divine command since, 'Among those we have created are a

community who guide by truth and by truth act with justice' (
Infallibility is a feature of it as the *hadith* (a saying of the Prophet
records, 'My community shall never agree upon an error; so if you
disagreement stay with the majority'.

A historical base can be seen in that the Muslim calendar dates from th
the *hijra* (Migration) from Mecca to Yathrib (later Medina) in the year A.D. 622.
Muhammad led those who accepted his preaching out of a city where blood-ties
formed the uniting bonds to establish a community built on faith, transcending such
former links.

The divine command and a complete way of life are the dominant features of the
Muslim understanding of the religious community. All life is to be lived in
submission to the will of God.

(d) Christianity: the Church

Three approaches are outlined only briefly here as information concerning the
breadth and richness of Christian organization and practice is widely available,
often through local examples.

The monastic tradition is strong amongst Roman Catholics, Orthodox Christians
and the Church of England. Founders and their Rules, the aims and work of the
various communities, and the differing emphases in preaching, nursing, con-
templative and other Orders allow a study of the religious life in historical and
modern times.

Patterns of church government provide another approach, noting how the
different denominations seek inspiration from the Holy Spirit through episcopal,
presbyterian and congregational structures. Ecumenical Councils, Synods and
Church Meetings give varying pictures of the relationships between clergy and
laity.

The Church as a serving agency is a third possibility with the work of the
Salvation Army or ecumenical activity through Christian Aid illustrating the social
and outward looking aspects of the Christian community.

Whilst this section could be so broad it is necessary to stress that no view of the
Christian Church could be complete which fails to note that its work has always
included both the preaching of the gospel and the healing of the sick (St Luke 9:2).

Work resulting from these studies can fit into two distinct and necessary
categories.

First, there is the opportunity to enlarge the technical vocabulary of religion,
particularly in respect of the relative titles of Christian clergymen, the different
religious communities and the historical background to many religious institutions.

Second, an appreciation of the manner and purpose of life within, for example,
the *Sangha*, Church or other community such as the Jewish nation should be
described in an extensive project which may include written, dramatised and tape-
recorded work. The child may attempt to explore the attitude and motivation of

monk, nun or layman, and seek to understand what beliefs prompt the activities he discovers.

(8) The Sacred Ganges

Under ideal conditions we would wish children to experience the practice of various faiths by actually visiting places where different rites are in daily use. Since we are normally unable to realize this aim save on the smaller scale of local visits we need to simulate such an encounter by building up a picture of life and worship at some centre which is of significance for more than one of the religions of the world. This final scheme employs the method of visiting a particular sacred site and noting the origin, meaning and expression of the practices found there.

The Indian sub-continent offers a view of Hinduism, Jainism, Buddhism, Christianity and Islam. The more specific area of the River Ganges is our more modest example, for even here is found a microcosm of Indian religious activity.

The Ganges, which flows through the north and north-east of India, is of major religious importance in the sub-continent and its various cities are strong in Hindu and Buddhist associations. Jainism also was once a feature of the same region.

As we build up a picture of this river and its environs, the aim is to help the children appreciate how and why faiths are practised in areas which are of great and living significance to their adherents.

(a) Purification

Running water is in almost universal use in religion to symbolize spiritual cleansing. This is the fundamental pattern and belief attaching to the Ganges which is in continual use by people undergoing ceremonial ablutions. The living bathe daily, at almost any place along its Indian length. The ascetic and devout stand for long periods meditating whilst immersed in its waters. The dead have Ganges water poured ceremonially into their mouths before cremation takes place. The water used in any Hindu temple for rituals of purification is preferably Ganges water, the river's presence and influence thus spreading throughout India.

(b) Mythology

The river itself is personified as the goddess Ganga whilst the total mythology attaching to the Ganges is rich and powerful. The river has its source at the foot of Vishnu, one of the great Gods and held to be the Preserver in addition to acting as an agent of creation. From there the Ganges' first heavenly course is as the Milky Way, and when the gods permit the stream to descend to earth its sheer bulk would have proved universally destructive had not Siva, the other great God of Hinduism who is, however, often cast as the Destroyer, caught the waters in his hair. Siva is often depicted in Hindu art as having great locks of hair, a traditional mark of the Indian holy man. The river's descent through Siva's hair is in seven streams to ensure the earth's safety, and it falls through the Himalayas which are the dwelling place of the gods and across the northern plains of India.

(c) Cities of Pilgrimage

The cities of Hardwar, where the Ganges reaches the plains, and Allahabad, which is further downstream, are centres of Hindu devotion. Vishnu's footprint, preserved in stone at Hardwar, is a popular site of pilgrimage. There is a similar relic at Gaya which lies below Banaras (or Benares). Where the river leaves the foothills Siva is worshipped as the Lord of the Mountains. In the summer months of May, June and July pilgrims journey six hundred miles downstream from Hardwar and Badrinath on the great Ganges pilgrimage, the exceptionally determined making the road journey prostrate. At Allahabad the Ganges is joined by another sacred river, the Jumna, and ritual bathing is common at this place of confluence.

(d) Banaras

Banaras is the most holy city in India. Mythology marks it as the meeting place of the three forms of the Ganges; the earthly river, the heavenly Milky Way, and the invisible or underground mythical stream. The city is full of temples, large and small, and holy men. Hindu worship does not follow any one particular form but it should involve the whole of oneself and the various senses in making an offering to the divine. Worship in Banaras is no different from that offered elsewhere but it is considered more efficacious.

Repetition of a divine name, the sweet scent of joss-sticks, the ringing of bells, dancing and the sharing of food offered to the gods are all, among other patterns also, elements in Hindu worship, whether in temple or home-shrine. Worship is normally an individual act, even when the devotee is in a temple. In Banaras it is continuous and dominant.

An excellent aid for this section is the Educational Productions Ltd film-strip *A Hindu Puja*, No. C6820. A tape recording is available for use with this strip.

(e) Buddhism

The city of Banaras is sacred to the Buddhists also. When Gautama Buddha preached his first sermon in the Deer Park there he set in motion the 'Wheel of the Doctrine'. Pictures and images of the Buddha in this position are frequent. He is seated and his hands form the symbolic gesture of 'turning the Wheel of the Doctrine', he is preaching the Truth. Sometimes gazelles adopt an attitude of worship, indicating the setting, whilst again the Buddha may be depicted being bathed before giving his sermon. The Wheel alone is sufficient to symbolize the Truth taught at Banaras, and because the association is historical this site is one of the four places connected with the Buddha's life and work most revered by Buddhists.

(f) Death

Hindu life is, ideally, divided into four stages. Whilst it is common for caste Hindus to accept the sacred thread and later to become householders, establishing their own families, few progress to the stages of *vanaprastha* (hermit) and the *sannyasin* (wandering holy man). Banaras in particular and the banks of the Ganges in general attract those who have broken all earthly ties and who wish to devote the final years of their present existence to seeking complete religious fulfilment. The pious live near the river, religious teachers are in evidence, cremations take place at the Burning Ghats at Banaras as the body is burned on a sandalwood pyre, and ashes are scattered on the river whether after Banaras funerary rites or whether pilgrims have brought the ashes of dead relatives to this sacred place from other parts of India. Ganga, Goddess of Purity, acknowledges the faithful and cleanses and receives at death.

(g) The Whole of Life

Worship, instruction, sacred ritual, pilgrimage, purification and funerary rites are all found at the Ganges. The teacher, devout, novice, ascetic, widow and priest all live by its banks. The river is in every home-shrine and every temple where water symbolizes purification. Indian religion, whether Hindu or Buddhist, seems not to exist without recourse to this dominant centre of pilgrimage and devotion.

A project file is only the starting point for work resulting from this approach. Obviously there is room and necessity for description, maps and diagrams depicting and explaining the geography, mythology and activity of Banaras and the Ganges.

Model making is also necessary in the construction of a replica of a Hindu shrine and its aids to devotion. Genuine figurines and copies of Hindu scriptures are obvious advantages.

Dance should be used to recreate and interpret the myths associated with the Ganges, to portray the pilgrimage or the hope of rebirth to a higher existence, and to depict the start of the Buddha's work of teaching.

To recapture the pattern of the original which is being studied it is necessary to employ full use of all the various human faculties and emotions, writing and description being joined by movement, music and colour.

Section Three
Introducing Literary Religious Symbols

Chapter 5
The Need and the Method

(1) The Need

We have maintained that in general artistic vehicles of communication are capable of providing insights in themselves without prior understanding of the forms employed being essential or even desirable.[1] Therefore it might be argued that a study of symbols and symbolic forms used in religious language, undertaken to discover what the writers were saying, should be unnecessary. The answer, however, lies in the fact that, despite the use of some symbolic devices in everyday living, in this materialistic, scientific, and technological age we no longer automatically appreciate literary symbols and myths or what they convey, even though (as we shall see) we readily employ metaphorical language in proverbial expressions.

For example, we do not need to understand the form of a piece of music to appreciate it or gain insights from it,[2] but to gain insights from any literary expressions and forms we must understand the spoken or written word.[3] It should be clear, therefore, that in educational terms any symbolic expressions and forms that are employed by a writer will need to be examined and appreciated, if the words which go to make up those expressions and forms are not to be misunderstood or ignored.

More specifically concerning religious language we can make virtually the same point. For the purpose of the argument, let us confine our thoughts to the more familiar Hebraic-Christian tradition. If we allow that understanding the Bible has an essential place in religious education (and a justification in practical terms will be given in the course of the discussion), then it is clear that teachers must understand the nature of this literature and, in turn, enable the children to understand also. Many of the religious or theological insights are expressed in symbols and through specific literary forms, while anything we say about God Himself must of necessity be through symbolic language, since He cannot be comprehended or described but only apprehended through experience. Thus, understanding of the symbolic forms and symbolic language in general is vital if the Bible is to be properly understood and appreciated on its own terms.

Against this, certain modern theologians[4] say that modern man has no need of myth and symbol and indeed, has grown out of both. We should, however, note three things:

(a) A biblical symbol is usually replaced by another metaphorical expression; for example, 'God up there' is replaced by 'Depth of existence', 'Ground of our Being', or 'Our ultimate concern'.[5]

(b) There is an assumption that we can successfully separate myth and symbol from history and that it is desirable to do so.

(c) We cannot avoid the fact that Biblical events took place at a particular time in a particular place. Moreover, the approach and methods employed by the Biblical authors and editors for writing history differed from ours. We certainly have to look at the Bible with artistic, Eastern eyes, rather than from a Western historical and scientific outlook, while in passing we should also note that in religious literature as a whole, even when considering examples by Western poets and other writers, we are largely concerned with Eastern expressions and ideas. In the first instance, at any rate, we must appreciate these facts, if we are not to misunderstand and misuse the scriptures and other writings.

The events themselves, of course, in Biblical history are according to faith relevant for all time and have a world-wide significance, and this underlines the value of the symbolic and mythological expressions as opposed to the use of purely historical statements.

Despite the implication of what was said in (b) above, we can nevertheless insist that when looking at many Biblical stories, particularly in the gospels, there is a need to realize that there is a difference between 'what happened' – the historical facts lying behind what is being recorded, and 'what was going on'[6] – the significance, the meaning, what the evangelists or other writers are really saying to us in the language of faith concerning their convictions derived from their experiences, and to see that what really matters to us is 'what was going on'.

If we appreciate this, then we will see that in many cases it is no longer so important to ask, 'Did it happen as described?', in a consideration of the miracles, for example. However, it is the symbolic and mythological expressions within the whole story, not separated from it, that give the timeless 'message' and show the significance of the event.

Apart from the desirability of being true to the literature itself in our use of it, and, indeed, fair to the authors, as a matter of principle, there are two practical considerations which reinforce this need for introducing the children to this symbolic language and mythological method of communication:

(i) Experience has shown that there is a real danger of children abandoning the Bible as a whole as untrue, once they discover that many stories, for example those in Genesis 1–11, do not stand up historically (as they understand it) or scientifically.

(ii) Even if the Bible as a whole is not abandoned, there is the danger nevertheless that they regard as 'true' only those parts which they consider historical, and disregard what they see as 'only myths', because symbolic forms and expressions are foreign to them when they think in Western historical and scientific terms, and consequently they miss much of what the Bible is really saying.

Further, unless these misconceptions are dealt with in the school years, they will often be rigidly held in adult life.

If these attitudes are to be avoided or dispelled before they can take root, our symbolic language training programme is best done within the 8–13 age range and reinforced in the later secondary years. This will also remove the need for the undesirable process of unlearning and relearning in a different way in a child's secondary school career.[7]

(2) The Method

On the surface, symbol and myth may appear to be far removed from the children's present-day experience. If, however, we approach the symbol in artistic terms, appreciating the natural affinity between religion and the arts and the fact that religion has always been communicated through artistic and symbolic means,[8] and we ensure that the aesthetic work of the school is being fully developed in every possible way,[9] coming to grips with the problems of religious language and symbols is not so formidable as it might seem.

We can certainly make the task easier by employing the sequences of artistic experiences approach, through which we can often present symbolic material in a context proper and natural to it, at the same time as we undertake the symbolic language training.[10] Our symbolic dance-drama work in particular will help the process of learning to think symbolically by the nature of the case.[11] Again, our task is simpler if the arts, including music and movement, various stories and fairy-tales, have been used liberally in infant religious education before the 'symbolic training' as such is undertaken.[12] Moreover, beginning to think symbolically also arises in learning from the experiences of others, when looking at the use of sacred places and buildings, or religious artistic expressions and activities, which we have seen is also an important area of work for the 8–13 age range.

We have already expressed the view that the method for introducing literary religious symbols in the middle school years involves going to the source of such symbols in religion itself, rather than making extensive use of secular-orientated schemes.[13] This does not preclude the use of one or two preliminary schemes in secular terms, such as looking at everyday signs and symbols, like traffic lights, road signs, the policeman as a symbol of law and order, and so on, but their use should be kept to a minimum. Normally, we should examine the employment of religious literary symbols in terms of the religious texts where they are found.

This does not mean that there will be little or no reference to the child's experience (as might also have been inferred from the opening remarks in this section on method), since the procedure, in fact, will often quite properly involve our looking at such symbols as they are used outside religion, particularly in respect of their employment in proverbial expressions.

The religious symbols when first employed could only work if they were living symbols,[14] and this could only happen if the metaphorical expressions used were drawn from everyday life or from the experiences and the history of the people. Thus, the use of the rock imagery in the Old and New Testaments, for example, as applied to God to express the idea of His reliability, steadfastness, trustworthiness, strength, and power (e.g. Ps. 18:2), and to Jesus in terms of His being the Foundation stone (Eph. 2:20, cf. St Matt. 7:25–27), was derived from the apparent permanence of rocks and mountains as far as everyday observation went, and the use of foundation stones in building, since the Biblical writers or the people for whom they wrote hardly thought in terms of modern geological findings![15] However, the same is still true for our children and for ourselves. Many of the old symbols are still alive. For example, in popular usage we too think of rocks being durable substances, while we employ expressions like, 'As firm' or 'As steady as a rock' or 'A rock-like character'.

Similarly, the water symbol arises out of the facts that water is both a necessity of life and conversely is often something to be feared (when thinking in terms of floods and oceans). The scarcity of water in the dry season in Palestine, moreover, added point to the use of water imagery in the two testaments in terms of longing for God and essential spiritual needs (Pss. 42:1, 63:1, and St John 4:1–15), while at the same time the Hebrews feared the sea, and this led naturally to the use of the image as a symbol of destruction and of impending death from whatever cause (Ps. 69:1 and St Mark 4:35–41), the ocean being the place where the great dragon and the demons lived (Amos 9:3; Ps. 104:26; Rev. 13:1; and cf. St Mark 5:13). In addition, the use of water for cleansing was readily applied in the acted symbols of ritual washings and baptismal rites and then metaphorically in literature (Ps. 51:2). These ideas, however, are not remote from the children's experiences, for we still need water to live, it can be a source of danger, and we use it for washing and cleaning.

When we introduce the religious symbols by considering their natural origins, we are not playing with secular symbolism. In the first place we are looking at the natural origins as natural, God-given phenomena and not as symbols. In the second place, what we are really doing, quite legitimately, is to go through the thought processes of the original writers. We are seeing why and how the symbols could be both readily employed and readily understood.

The procedure for working is best seen from the schemes themselves in the next chapter. Before we look at these, it is desirable to conclude our present remarks with a further word about introducing myth as a form.

It is vital that when we apply our Western criticism to such material, we put back what we take away. In other words, we should never use, or allow our pupils to use, the words 'only' or 'just' with the words 'a myth'. We even need to qualify such a phrase as 'this story is not historically true'.[16]

One simple way of approaching the Genesis 3–11 myths, for example, is to see them as timeless, Everyman parables. Let the children see that there are many 'towers of Babel' in politics and big business today. Let them see that all men walk in their 'gardens of Eden' in the sense that all have to decide between right and wrong, even though technically we might insist that we are all now in the wilderness of the world, just as Jesus was tempted in the desert. Similarly, the solar mythology of the Samson Saga (Judges 14–16)[17] can be appreciated as an Old Testament version of the New Testament idea contained in the parable of the Talents (St Matthew 25:14–30). In other words, we borrow a term from another important religious language form to help us understand the myths.

Alternatively, we may prefer to use the idea of 'picture-language' instead of that of the parable. Certainly, many children readily understand the term, which does not destroy the truth underlying the language, but warns against taking the words in question too literally, and, moreover, does not presuppose the knowledge of another literary form.

Notes

1. See pp. 4–7, 8ff, above.
2. See pp. 8–9 above.
3. We saw earlier how this will affect our choice of material from literature for artistic sequences – see p. 10 above.
4. By no means all: see, e.g. Mircea Eliade, *Myth and Reality*, Harper and Row, 1963, *The Two and the One*, Harvill, latest English Edition 1965, *Myths, Dreams and Mysteries*, Fontana, latest English Edition 1968; T. Fawcett, *The Symbolic Language of Religion*, SCM Press, 1970, and *Hebrew Myth and Christian Gospel*, SCM Press, 1973; I. T. Ramsay, *Religious Language*, SCM Press, 1957, *Models and Mystery*, OUP, 1964, *Christian Discourse*, OUP, 1965.
5. So Paul Tillich, *The Shaking of the Foundations*, SCM Press, 1949, also available in a Pelican-Penguin paperback, and *The New Being*, SCM Press, 1956. Tillich, of course, does see the value and importance of the symbol, and, indeed, of myth, and his writings – including his *Systematic Theology* – can properly be added to the list of note 4 above.
6. Cf. John Marsh, *Saint John*, Pelican Gospel Commentaries, Penguin, 1968, p. 18.
7. We raised the problem concerning introducing symbolic and mythological material in sequences for very young children before the symbolic language training could reasonably take place on p. 7 above with discussion on the issue on pp. 7–8, and 9–12. All that we are saying here is that we should certainly avoid the drastic, and often traumatic, unlearning and relearning process in the secondary years, particularly as it is so unnecessary.
8. See p. 1 above.
9. See p. 15 above.
10. Cf. and contrast pp. 8 and 10 above, where the point is made the other way round, i.e. it is less difficult to appreciate symbolic material in artistic sequences if the symbolic language training is underway. Each procedure, of course, helps the other. See also p. 15 above.
11. See p. 13 above.
12. Cf. pp. 3, note 3 cont., 10, and 13 above.
13. See p. 2 note 3 above.
14. Cf. T. Fawcett, *The Symbolic Language of Religion*, op. cit., p. 27.
15. Moreover, for practical purposes, considering a reasonable span of time, geologists themselves are employed to ensure that buildings, roads, and railways, etc., are constructed on firm foundations of rock or advise a sound man-made subsititute, as the example on 'The Rock' (see pp. 100–104) will show.
16. Cf. pp. 11–12 above.
17. The solar elements are found in these chapters, the saga itself beginning with an introduction by editors concerned with reforms in the eighth century B.C., who were also responsible for the Book of Deuteronomy in its present form. The story of Samson is based on the Babylonian Gilgamesh epic and has parallels too with the tales of Hercules of Greek mythology, though in the Hebrew story Samson is clearly a man and not a demi-god and the tale is set in a genuine historical framework, revealing the uneasy co-existence between the Danites and the Philistines, either before the Danite migration, or concerning those Danites who chose to stay behind after their fellow Danites had moved. The solar traits are as follows:

   (a) Samson's name is derived from the Hebrew word for the sun, in turn, derived from the Babylonian god Shamash.
   (b) Samson's strength lies in the rentention of his hair – seven locks 16:13 = the seven rays of the sun

– his weakness is due to its loss (16:17). This solar element is disguised by the editorial device of making Samson a Nazirite.

(c) He slays a lion singlehanded (14:5ff); cf. Hercules story, though in itself this would not be an impossible feat, but the point can be used in support of the others.

(d) The burning of the foxes' tails=the red blight on the corn (15:1ff); cf. the Roman Ceres festival.

(e) He leaves the city of Gaza at dawn, carrying its gate, which probably faced east, and the posts to the top of the hill before Hebron (16:3)=sun rising.

(f) Hot springs were sacred to Hercules. Samson is conveniently revived by them (=spring after winter weakness) (15:18ff).

(g) At the end of the tale he grinds the corn by treading the wheel (16:21) (=the sun tracing its daily path), and brings down the pillars of the temple, i.e. the seven pillars holding up the heavens, and is destroyed together with the Philistines (16:28ff), the carnage representing the setting of the sun, and, in fact, the sun's destruction, as in some versions of the solar myth – as in Homer (Greek), for example.

Chapter 6
Examples

Thomas Fawcett and John K. Thornecroft

In this chapter we shall confine our examples to the Hebraic-Christian tradition for the following reasons:

1. Western children (including those from the West Indian populace) probably need the training in symbolic language more than their Eastern contemporaries.
2. It is easier for teachers and Western children alike to come to grips with religious language through what is for them the more familiar tradition.
3. Bibles are readily available, as are commentaries and guides on the text. Literature of the other world religions is not so easily obtainable, particularly for use by the class as a whole.
4. Once the method or approach is grasped, however, it can be readily applied, if desired, to some examples from the literature of world religions. In such cases teachers will normally have to prepare copies of the chosen extracts for the children. If required, permission to reproduce the passages concerned should be obtained from the appropriate authority.

Following the policy of the contributors of chapter 4 we shall concentrate on illustrating the procedure for the task in hand – in this case providing training in religious language, and on the selection of suitable material, and the content, order, and arrangement of that material, while again with non-specialist teachers particularly in mind endeavouring to supply sufficient information and guidance to remove the need for too much additional research and reading on the part of the teacher when time and energies are at a premium.

Therefore we also have taken the view that it is right to leave the teacher with considerable scope regarding appropriate children's activities for his particular class, although some suggestions for children's work are given by way of exemplifying the kind of work that can be done. Nevertheless, for these schemes it will be clear that we consider Bible-study and class or group discussions are particularly appropriate throughout.

Finally, although in the last chapter we said that the symbolic training should take place in the middle school years, it will be seen that the last two schemes (nos. 7 and 8) in their entirety are more suitable for the older secondary children because of the nature of the material for the concluding discussions. Even so, sections of 'The Prophets as Teachers', and the main ideas and approach of the 'Water' scheme, can be used with children aged 12–13.

(1) **Animals**

The aim in this scheme is to introduce the idea of symbolism. We begin immediately to use it as a means of understanding and also lay a foundation for future work.

(a) Different Kinds of Animals

With the aid of pictures or slides the children identify various animals and learn some simple facts about them.

The various animals can then be placed into different groups. A card, preferably showing a picture, can be made of each animal, and a set of animals given to each child. They are then asked to divide their animals into two groups, all the tame animals in one and all the wild animals in the other. When their choices have been checked, the children write lists of tame and wild animals from their two piles of cards. The same procedure can be followed to divide the large from the small animals, the fast from the slow, and so on. In this way a knowledge of the characteristics of various animals is built up.

(b) Animals Have Characters

Using the cards again the children try to find words to describe each animal, choosing one which seems to describe it best. The teacher then explains that many animals are noted for certain characteristics and that human beings who behave in certain ways are often compared to animals which are thought of as behaving in these ways. For example: as crafty as a fox; as nimble as a goat; as big as an elephant; as strong as an ox; as stubborn as a mule; as noble as a horse; as lowly as a donkey. The sayings may be written up on the blackboard with the adjectives left out for the children to supply.

(c) The Horse and the Donkey

The differences between a horse and a donkey are explored. This can be helped by the use of Aesop's fable about the Horse and the Ass in which the horse refused to bear any of the burden so that the ass eventually died from exhaustion with the result that the horse, instead of sharing the load, had to carry the whole burden and the dead donkey's skin as well.

We go on to find that the horse has always been regarded as a noble animal and has been the steed of kings and emperors. The donkey on the other hand has been despised and regarded as the poor man's animal. We can demonstrate with pictures the use of the horse in war and pageantry. In contrast we find that the donkey is used in the gospel story, first by Joseph and Mary according to tradition for their flight into Egypt (Christmas cards will illustrate this well), and then by Jesus when He entered Jerusalem on Palm Sunday. The children must be helped to see why Jesus deliberately used a donkey instead of a horse and was careful to arrange for this (St Mark 11:1–10). Two useful aids are 'Three Donkeys', a record of stories told by David Kossoff and 'The Donkey', a poem by G. K. Chesterton.

(d) The Lion and the Lamb

We explore the differences between the lion and the lamb in a similar way but concentrate now on the heraldic use of animals. We can begin by looking at some heraldic devices and noting the way in which men have chosen animals as part of the design which will represent them and their families.

The story of Richard I can be told briefly, followed by a discussion as to why he was called the 'Lionheart'. The idea of Jesus as the Lamb can be introduced by one or more of the many pictures which show a lamb to represent Jesus or in which Jesus is accompanied by a lamb. It is too early in the symbolic training process to explain the connection of the lamb with sacrifice, but the character of the lamb as harmless to other animals, etc., can be shown to be appropriate.

The scheme can be concluded by each child being asked to design a shield to represent someone they know about, and to use on it whatever animal they think would be best.

(2) **Trees**

Under this heading three schemes are given for the age-ranges 8–9, 9–11, and 12–13 respectively on the subject of the symbolism of trees. The arrangement is intended to show how the nature of religious language can be introduced and developed during these years. The three schemes therefore give an outline course on similes and metaphors, parables and allegories.

(a) Countries and Their Trees (8–9)

We begin by discovering that certain trees come to be associated with the country in which they flourish. As we cannot do very much with maps at this stage it will be best to restrict ourselves to just one or two examples.

(i) **The Maple of Canada**
The sugar maple is native to North America and was adopted as the national emblem of Canada. We study a picture of the maple tree, find out some of its uses, and discover where Canada is. This can be followed by reading or singing Canada's national song: 'The Maple Leaf for Ever'.

(ii) The Almond
This was common in Palestine and was used as a national emblem for a time. Just before the time of Jesus, in the Maccabean period when the Jews had their own native rulers, the almond was represented on their basic coin, the shekel. This can be linked with the story of Judas in which the reference is probably to such coins (St Matthew 26:15).

(iii) The Balsam of Judaea
We introduce the facts that the balsam tree grew in southern Palestine where Jesus lived, it was rare, and so its products were very expensive and prized. When the Romans under Pompey conquered the country this was among the spoils carried off to Rome. The story of the anointing of Jesus with oil of the balsam tree can be told and acted out at this point by way of illustration (St Matthew 26:6–13).

(b) The Character of Trees (9–11)

We now look at any convenient number of trees in order to see that each one has its own special character. The children are asked to suggest words with which to describe each tree and so build up a few pen-pictures.

(i) The Oak
We notice the large, firm roots, its great girth, and so its appearance of strength and stability. We read or sing the eighteenth-century song about the British ships made from its timber – 'Heart of Oak Are Our Ships'. We see how the men in the ships are also compared with oak trees.

(ii) The Weeping Willow
We study a picture of the tree and try to find out why it was given this name.

(iii) The Pine
The children are reminded of the carol 'Good King Wenceslas' and find out what tree is mentioned in it and why 'pine logs' were chosen – because pine wood burns readily.

Point out that the names of some trees are really descriptions of some outstanding feature.

(i) The Almond
The name means 'to keep watch' because its pink and white flowers opened before the leaves at the end of January and the beginning of February, so seeming to keep watch for the spring and herald it with its flowers (Jer. 1:11).

(ii) The Palm
This tree was called *palma* which is Latin for 'hand', because the leaves which are fan or feather-shaped radiate like fingers of an outstretched hand.

(iii) The Cedar
The Jews used a word for this tree (*erez*) which meant 'firmly rooted and strong'.

(c) Trees (12–13)

From this more advanced work on trees the children should: learn more about the way analogies work by seeing them used in parables and allegories; find out more about the country which produced our Bible; acquire a broad outline of biblical history.

(i) People Compared with Trees
The idea of comparison is introduced and then followed up by showing the way in which a number of comparisons can be put together to make a parable or allegory. Scholars attempt to use these terms to refer to two different kinds of story. A parable is used for stories which are simple, need no explanation, and generally make just one point. They are designed to make people think. They demand a decision or ask a question. An allegory, on the other hand, is usually held to be a story in which each person or incident is a parallel to a person or event in real history. Scholars, however, are not unanimous in their use of these terms, and there are cases, particularly in the Old Testament, where given the above 'definitions' the two forms appear to be mixed within the same story. It would seem best therefore not to belabour a point which children find difficult to understand. For our purposes, at least, it is generally sufficient to ensure that a parable (pure and simple) is not made to say more than was intended.

A *Jewish Ideals*
We can introduce our subject by using two simple examples:

1. The ideal prosperity for which a Jew looked is described in Psalm 128, which is short enough to be studied as a whole. With some help from the teacher the children are able to see from it what a Jew valued most in life. In doing this two comparisons with trees will be mastered from verse 3.
2. From Psalm 1:1–3 the children can learn what a Jew regarded as a good man and see why a tree made an effective comparison.

B *The Making of a King*
The teacher must explain that three trees are constantly mentioned by the Jews – the olive, the fig, and the vine – because they were the three most valuable trees they used. The reasons for this can be examined briefly here by listing the products from these trees which the Jews used.

The story found in Judges 9:1–21 is best told by the teacher, except for the fable of Jotham in verses 7–15 which provides suitable material for a dance-mime. This parable is considered in the light of the story, and the children discover why Jotham compares the noble sons of Jerubbaal (Gideon) to the good trees in the land and Abimelech to a bramble.

Historical Note

Up to the end of the period of the Judges (*c.* 1020 B.C.), the people of Israel considered that God was their King and that no human ruler should reign over them, i.e. Israel was a theocratic entity. When the Philistines, the sea-peoples who had settled on the western coast, first drove the tribe of Dan northwards, taking over its territory, and then became a threat to the whole of Israel, a monarchy became a military necessity, and it seems from 1 Samuel 8 that many Israelites had a change of heart and wanted a human king like other nations.

Nevertheless, one of the two accounts of the anointing of Saul as the first king (1 Sam. 8:1–22 and 10:17–27; cf. 9:1–10:1) shows Samuel's reluctance for Israel to have a human monarch. Although the narrative reflects later reactions to the evils that occurred in the reigns of Solomon and his son Rehoboam, it may still indicate that there were, in fact, many at the end of the period of the Judges who regarded the move towards a monarchy as a false step. At least it is clear that when David was to succeed Saul (*c.* 1000) religious leaders, represented by Nathan the prophet, saw the importance of maintaining that God was still the real King of Israel (2 Sam. 7, cf. 5:1–5). The problem was solved by making the king the adopted son of God, invested with His power and authority (2 Sam. 7:8–16). Eventually, Psalm 2, which contained an adoption formula (verse 7), was used on the day of the king's enthronement.

Although in the period of the Judges Gideon, Abimelech's father, was offered the crown in a moment of enthusiasm and gratitude for what he had done for them, the people were not really ready to accept the idea of human kingship, and thus Gideon refused the crown and promised that his son would not rule over them either (Judges 8:22–23). Judges 9, however, shows that Abimelech made a bid for kingship by removing any other possible claimants (9:1–5 and 18), and having himself made king over his mother's clan, the Shechemites (9:18).

Note on the Literary Form

The fable of Jotham (9:7–15) is a parable, because it demands a reaction and a decision to be made by the hearers, with allegorical details, the noble sons being compared to the good trees and Abimelech to the bramble. Its main point is that among humans only the worthless have time to rule, with the implication that only God can be King over Israel. But there is a further thought. If they must have a king, let them make sure that they make the right choice. The stupidity of accepting Abimelech is expressed in stronger terms and described as an absurdity by the idea that the large trees can be sheltered by the lower growing shrub.

C   *A Quarrel Between Kings*

We now go on to see how an allegory was used in an attempt to persuade a king not to start a war. The whole story is found in 2 Kings 14:1–14. The following chart can be used to show how the allegory parallels the events which will take place if the war starts.

The History	*The Allegory*
Amaziah of Judah sends a message to Jehoash of Israel asking to be treated as an equal.	A thistle sends a message to a cedar asking for a marriage between their children.
The army of Jehoash defeats Amaziah at the battle of Bethshemesh and despoils Jerusalem.	A wild beast tramples down the thistle.

(ii) Two Great Nations Compared with Trees

We now see how two great empires of Old Testament times were compared to trees. This introduces the Egyptian and Babylonian Empires which played such an important part in Israelite history and also paves the way for later sections when we find the nation of Israel compared to a tree.

A map of the Near East is essential to show how Palestine was placed between the two great powers, Egypt to the south and Babylon to the north-east. The teacher should explain that the people of Israel were constantly caught in the fights between these two kingdoms and were often subject to one of them.

A   *Egypt the Cedar* (Ezekiel 31)

The power and importance of Egypt in Old Testament times is explained and illustrated.

Ezekiel 31:2–9 contains a poem in which Egypt is compared to a Cedar of Lebanon. This can be studied in detail and the class encouraged to see what features of the tree the poet finds expressive of Egypt at the height of its glory. Points which might be made are: the size of Egypt and its Empire; its pride so that its head was 'among the clouds'; the importance of the Nile to its life and prosperity; its influence over other peoples; the wealth of the country on which other people sometimes had to rely; the advanced state of Egyptian civilization – its buildings and art.

Verses 10–18 contain a judgment on Egypt given by the prophet in the name of God. If it is desired to follow this up by a discussion, the glory of Egypt must be seen to have been brought about at the expense of much human misery – for this the nation is condemned. It should be noticed that this passage contains a number of poetic allusions which cannot be understood readily at this age and are best omitted in this scheme (references to the Pit or Sheol, and the Garden of Eden). Understanding the reference to Sheol, for example, is not essential for understanding the use of the Tree imagery. In Scheme 7, 'The Prophets as Teachers', the Sheol doctrine has to be tackled in order that Amos 9:2 can be appreciated – see p. 117 below. In any case Scheme 7 as a whole is recommended for use with older secondary children, see p. 89 above.

B   *Nebuchadrezzar's* Dream of a Tree* (Dan. 4)

In Daniel 4 we find Nebuchadrezzar's Babylon compared to a tree in much the

---

* Following the more correct spelling of Jeremiah, as compared with that of the Chronicler and the author of Daniel.

same way as Ezekiel compared Egypt to the cedar. Verses 10–17 give the allegory as it appears in the king's dream and verses 20–26 give the interpretation.

The point must be made that this is a complete allegory and the dream and its interpretation can be placed side by side, an exercise which the abler children might attempt for themselves.

Finally, the purpose of the allegory should be made clear as expressed in verse 27.

Note

Scholars have observed that originally this tale probably referred to Nabonidus, the last king of Babylon (555–539 B.C.), on the basis of a prayer by Nabonidus found in a Dead Sea Scroll. A Jew came to the king while he was ill at Tema, and warned him about worshipping idols, and encouraged him to worship the one true God.

The legends of Daniel 1–6, written down in their present form *c*. 167 at the time of the Maccabean revolt, were told many times among those Jews who lived in various parts of the Persian Empire after the fall of Babylon to Cyrus, the Persian, and who did not return to Judah when permission was granted them.

The legends were then later used to show that it is God who controls the fortunes of nations, raising them up and destroying them. No human king can be ruler of all the earth (Dan. 4:25), as ancient kings often made themselves out to be (cf. 4:1). Although we compare the tree with the Babylonian Empire, when we consider the historical situation, in the dream the tree symbolizes the whole earth (4:20), reflecting the king's attitude.

The particular purpose of this allegory as expressed in verse 27 is to make the king repent and act with mercy as a ruler (note that the function of a parable is present and that we really have another example of the mixing of the forms), but the story also emphasizes the main purpose of chapters 1–6 as a whole, since in 4:25–26 the king is encouraged to realize his real position in comparison with the true Ruler of the world, and that it is the Most High who is King of all men.

(iii) The Vine

The imagery of the vine is particularly useful. It gives a broad outline of biblical history. It was used both by the prophets and by Jesus as a means of expressing important religious ideas.

A   *The Vine brought out of Egypt*

A brief introduction is useful to explain the process of planting a new tree, noting how carefully this has to be done and what provisions have to be made for its future health. The point will then be understood later that the psalmist sees Israel as the object of God's very great care.

Psalm 80:8–18 sets out this idea in some detail. This psalm was probably written at the time of the downfall of the kingdoms of Israel and Judah and looks back over the history of Israel, interpreting it through the analogy of the vine. Israel is compared with a vine which is brought out of Egypt by God and planted in Palestine, in ground which God had prepared for it. In this way the model is related to the initiatory act whereby Israel became God's nation and to the Hebrew view of Canaan as a land which had been destined for it by God. The metaphor is then extended to indicate the way in which the nation prospered in Canaan and stretched from the Great Sea (the Mediterranean) to the Jordan, planting its roots deep in the land. The glories of the Davidic Kingdom, however, did not last and the wall around the vineyard of Israel was broken down by invading armies and marauding nomads so that in the time of the psalmist the land is desolated. This too is regarded as the work of the Lord, but the psalmist does not lose hope but calls upon God to give the nation back its life.

With the aid of the above summary the teacher can help the class to set out the allegory and its interpretation in parallel columns. Understanding can also be furthered by its use as a basis for art work, there being two word pictures provided – the prosperity of the vine and its subsequent destruction.

B   *The Products of the Vine*

The various products of the vine should be examined and this can then be followed by a study of the way in which the prophets spoke of the vine having become useless.

Deut. 32:32f. This passage condemns Israel and says that its fruit has become poisonous.

Hos. 10:1. Hosea tells the people that although God nurtured this vine, its fruit is the worship of idols, causing the social evils among the people.

Jer. 2:21. Jeremiah tells them that the vine which was grown from pure seed has gone wild.

Ezek.15:2, 6 Ezekiel points out that when there is no fruit on a vine, its wood is useless for the carpenter and fit only to be burnt.

Isa. 5:1–7 This passage summarizes much of the prophetic teaching. The verses which follow list further evils which Isaiah regarded as bad fruit.

These passages should form the basis on which the class can make a list of the evils which the prophets condemned as bad fruits. In order to bring out a fuller understanding of what the prophets were saying, however, it is useful that the pupils should consider their own country as a vine and suggest what good and bad fruits it has produced and is producing.

Note on Isaiah's Song of the Vineyard (Isa. 5:1–7)

This song may have been composed for the Feast of the Tabernacles during the reign of Jotham. The prophet imitates a popular vintage festival song. The identification given in verse 7 shows that it is an allegory, while at the same time the question demanding a judgment by the people on themselves in verse 4 shows that the passage is also a parable, so that yet again we have a mixed form here.

The care which the owner of the vineyard has taken in cultivating the vine is to be compared with the love and care God had already shown to His people in delivering them from slavery in Egypt, establishing a covenant with them on Mt Sinai, and giving them a land. He had also sent them judges – military captains and leaders – to protect them from invaders, and granted them kings, so that the Philistines could be defeated and the nation firmly established.

God expected the people of later ages to respond to His activity on behalf of the nation throughout their history, so that the good fruits would be good behaviour and lives consistent with the Will of God, not because they would be punished if they broke their side of the covenant, but out of gratitude for what God had already done for them (cf. Amos 2:9–11). However, the eighth century was an age of feudalism. The poor were exploited by the rich and corruption in the courts made it impossible for them to find true justice (Amos 2:7; 4:1; 5:12, etc.).

Though the motive for responding to God should have been one of gratitude and not fear of punishment, the result of their ingratitude, the poem makes clear, is nevertheless inevitable judgment and retribution, and in history these were expressed in terms of the two exiles, one for the North and one for the South (c. 721 and 586 B.C. respectively).

C   *The Unfaithful Vine* (Ezek. 17)

Ezekiel uses the imagery of the vine to state his attitude towards the political events at the time of the southern exile. The allegory is given in verses 3–10 and the explanation in verses 12–18. These can easily be set side by side, either by the teacher on the blackboard or as an exercise for the children. Having completed this, an attempt should be made to discover how Ezekiel chose his parallels very carefully. It should be noted how appropriate are the images of the great eagle, the city of merchants, and that of the well-watered land.

D   *The Wicked Husbandmen*

The leaders of Israel, Judah, and the later Jews were sometimes thought of as the husbandmen of the vineyard which belonged to God. This is done to show that the husbandmen have not always carried out their responsibilities or been loyal to the owner of the vineyard.

Isa. 3:14–15 speaks of the elders and princes as plunderers of the vineyard because they have become rich at the expense of the poor.

St Mark 12:1–12 contains the well-known parable of Jesus which can be understood more fully in the light of what has now been done. We must note that this story, although called a parable, is somewhat like an allegory (and is thus regarded as quite unique in the New Testament as opposed to the Old by many scholars) in that it is again possible to set out the story and its interpretation in parallel columns, and it is natural to see Jesus in the son of the owner, particularly from this side of the cross-resurrection experience.

E   *The New Vine and New Workers in the Vineyard*

Finally, we consider two ideas which are very important in the New Testament:

First, the vine is no longer a race of people, the Jews (or Ancient Israel in the light of our earlier considerations), but a community of faith and brotherhood centred on Jesus. This is expressed in the allegory of the vine in St John 15. Here is an opportunity to show how Jesus refused to confine the chosen people to the Jews, but expressed a new idea of man's relationship with God which had nothing to do with blood or race. (Cf. St Paul's use of the imagery of the olive in Romans 11:17–23.)

Second, in His parable of the labourers in the vineyard Jesus teaches that this new community is not made up of people who think they can earn the approval of God, but of all those who respond to His invitation (St Matthew 20:1–16).

(iv) The Fig Tree
The use of the imagery of the Fig Tree is similar to that of the vine, but there is a feature in its use which we have not met before and is more difficult to handle – the symbolism is not merely expressed in words but is acted out.

A *A Symbol of Prosperity*
Deut. 8:7–10 gives a description of the land to which God was bringing the Israelites from Egypt (though, of course, in retrospect). The passage is worth studying in some detail so that the children are able to list from it the features of the country which the Israelites valued. Amongst these was the presence of the fig tree. This is followed by a discussion on the value of the fig tree. It took a long time to cultivate, but men were rewarded for their efforts by the food (1 Sam. 30:11–12) and medicine (2 Kings 20:7) it provided.

B *Peace and War*
The days of Solomon's reign were largely peaceful and this is characterized in 1 Kings 4:25 by saying that every man was able to live safely under his vine and under his fig tree – a recurring image of pastoral serenity in the Old Testament.

In time of war the precious fig trees were destroyed. Joel 1 paints a picture of complete devastation in the countryside, probably after the disasters of the Assyrian and Babylonian invasions had left the country in a poor state. The fate of the fig tree and other trees is particularly mentioned (vv. 7, 12).

Consequently, whenever a prophet wished to speak of a good period of prosperity to come he frequently referred to a restoration of a time when 'every one of you will invite his neighbours under his vine and under his fig tree' (Zech. 3:10).

C *A Sign of Spring*
The Song of Solomon 2:10–13 gives a picture of the coming of spring in which the fig tree figures. (Cf. Jer. 1:11 and the use of the 'Almond' play on words referred to in the last scheme.)

St Mark 13:28 uses the fig as an example of the way men need to look to the events of their time and so be ready for what is to come.

D *Israel the Fig Tree*
Against the background we have now studied, it is possible to see how the fig was used as a symbol for Israel (or Judah), first in the Old Testament and then in the New.

Hosea 9:10 compares the beginnings of the Israelite nation to the first fruit of a new fig tree.

In Jeremiah, however, we find the prophet saying that there were good and bad figs in Judah. To Jeremiah the best figs, the cream of Judah's leadership, had been taken to Babylon, and only the bad figs had been left behind in Palestine (Jer. 24:1–10).

It is just the idea which lies behind these two passages which comes to the fore in the story of the withering of the fig tree in the gospel story (St Mark 11:12–14; 20–23).

St Luke 13:6–9 contains a parable which Jesus told about a fig tree. It is clear that the tree stands for the Jewish people in the parable and some have suggested that the three years in which it has failed to produce fruit is a reference to the three year ministry of Jesus to which the Jews have not responded. If this suggestion is correct, then Israel has its last chance with the final coming to Jerusalem of Jesus its King.

The theme is followed up in the story of the withering of the fig tree in St Mark 11:12–14; 20–23. This raises a number of difficulties. Some think that it has been developed out of the parable in St Luke and inserted in the earlier gospel. Others believe that Jesus has acted out the symbolism of the parable. What is clear, however, is that the fate of the fig tree here is intended to parallel the Jewish nation at this time. This can be shown best by the use of columns.

The Fig Tree	*The History*
The tree fails to provide fruit over three years (St Luke 13:6–7).	Jesus finds the Jewish nation failing to show the virtues of love and care demanded by God.
The tree has many leaves on it and so looks healthy from a distance (St Mark 11:13).	The Jews make a show of outward observance of religion.
There is, however, no fruit.	The will of God is not done.
The fig tree is withered (St Mark 11:21).	The nation stands under judgment and faces destruction for its sins.

(3) The Rock

The imagery of the rock spans the Old and New Testaments. This is useful because it avoids the usual fragmentation caused by the concentration on isolated elements within the history. It is fundamentally a simple image and can therefore be introduced at an early stage. Moreover, we can ground much of the work in the experience of the children (see pp. 85–86 above). It must be noted that only a selection of the biblical material is used. Some must be omitted, e.g. 1 Cor. 10:4, because reference to it at this stage would only cause confusion.

(a) Rocks and God

(i) The Characteristics of Rocks

We begin simply with a study of rocks, seeing and handling specimens, talking about the work of geologists, and becoming generally familiar with the variety of rock formations which exist. Reference can be made to the importance of collecting samples from the moon's surface or from deep within the earth's crust in order to discover layers of water, oil, or valuable minerals. We can also notice the importance of the geologist's work in the construction of motorways and railways.

(ii) The Hills of Palestine

The rocky nature of much of Palestine can be illustrated with photographs, slides, and film-strips. Reference can be made to the way in which the Jews of today have had to spend much time clearing the land of rocks in order to develop agriculture (cf. St Matthew 13:5). A physical map or model of Palestine is useful here to show how the country has a line of hill-country running down the centre like a backbone.

In order to appreciate how the Hebrews feel about the rocky hills, we must note their place in Hebrew history. This need only be done in outline to bring out the fact that the hill-country was frequently the area in which they took refuge in times of invasion. This is probably best illustrated by the story of the Maccabean rebellion.

In the second century (B.C.) the Syrian overlords of Palestine attempted to impose the worship of Greek idols on the Jews and placed one in the Temple at Jerusalem. The resistance to this movement began in a village called Modin where the family of Mattathias refused to sacrifice to the idols, killed the king's officer, and fled to the hills. The lead was taken by one of the sons of Mattathias, Judas, who came to be known as Maccabeus, the Hammerer, because he was so successful in his exploits against the Syrians. The revolt was eventually successful, the people freed from Syrian rule, and the Temple restored to its proper use. (The story of these events can be found in the Apocrypha, 1 Maccabees.)

The hill fighting of the Maccabees can be compared to modern examples of what is known as guerrilla warfare and the point grasped that the hills could be a place of refuge in times of trouble.

(iii) The Rock-like God

We are now in a position to understand why the Hebrews often referred to God as being like a rock. The idea is used constantly in simile or metaphor of God in the psalms, but it should be noted that the English translators have often given the meaning of the metaphor and not the original word, 'rock'. We frequently find, therefore, that words like 'refuge', 'strength', and so on, have been substituted for the Hebrew word 'rock'. Three passages from the psalms are probably sufficient for the purposes of illustration.

Psalm 18:1–2   The children are asked to make a list of all the words in the passage which are used to describe God. The teacher can then show how each one complements the others and builds up a picture of God as One whom the psalmist felt protected him from all evil.

Psalm 31:2–5   The class tries to find out what picture the psalmist has in mind and discovers that God is here thought of as a kind of castle in which the psalmist is saved from the traps laid for him by his enemies.

Psalm 62:1–8   The class can now spot familiar images which usually accompany that of the rock and see the strength of the psalmist's faith in the face of hypocrisy and lies.

(b) The City Built on a Rock

(i) The Capital City

With the aid of pictures and maps we learn about the site on which Jerusalem was built. We see why this ancient Jebusite stronghold was chosen by David as his capital (once he had discovered a way of capturing it). It was easy to defend because it was built on a hill, and it was in the centre of the land. The story of the unsuccessful siege of Sennacherib of Assyria illustrates its defensive strength (Isa. cs. 36 and 37; 2 Kings 18:13–20:19).

An outline of the history of Jerusalem can be included at this point, if desired, to show the importance of this city from a military point of view (see Historical Note appended to the scheme). This has the advantage of bringing our study into relationship with recent events in Palestine and the conflict between the Jews and the Arabs today.

(ii) The Temple on the Rock

The Rock of Jerusalem became the religious centre of Judaism. 2 Samuel 24:18–25 tells the story of how David purchased the site of the future temple from Araunah. At that time it was used as a threshing floor – the necessity of a stone surface for this purpose can be explained. 1 Kings cs. 5–8 continue the story showing how Solomon built the Temple on the site of the threshing floor.

(iii) Processions

As the centre of Hebrew religious life, Jerusalem and its temple became a centre of pilgrimage, especially for the three great feasts. Isa. 30:29 is a valuable verse at this point because it states briefly the essential features of these frequent processions to Jerusalem. It stresses the joy of such occasions and has a play on words – 'mountain' and 'rock'.

The verse is next compared with the story of Jesus' triumphal entry into Jerusalem (St Mark 11:1–11), which was in fact a procession to the temple.

Finally, Psalm 24 lends itself admirably to antiphonal speaking which may be combined with mime if space is available. One way of doing this is as follows:

The class is divided into three groups; a large group, A, constitutes the crowd lining the processional route; group B, fairly small, represents the priests inside the temple; group C represents the pilgrims approaching the temple. The words are spoken as follows:

A vv. 1–2   A. v. 8, lines b and c
B v. 3   C v. 9
A vv. 4–5   B v. 10, line a
C vv. 6–7   A and C v. 10, lines
B v. 8, line a   b and c

(c) Christ the Firm Foundation

(i) The Importance of Firm Foundations

At this point we should note the importance of sound foundations in all building projects. Attention is drawn to the choice of a site which will make a good base and particularly that architects prefer to build upon a stratum of rock. The folly of choosing a poor site can be illustrated from incidents in which a new housing estate has been built too near a crumbling coast-line. We observe that modern technology enables us to build on sandy or marshy ground, but that this can only be done when a substitute for rock is provided in the form of concrete or another suitable alternative.

(ii) Jesus the Rock

We see first how Jesus used this as an illustration in St Matthew 7:24–27 to make the point that men can only stand up to the storms of life if their actions are founded on the Will of God. To the Christian the Will of God for men's lives is shown in the life of Christ, and so for them Jesus is the example which they follow.

Here, the teacher must be prepared to discuss the character of Christ's life in order to bring out the fact that, although all sorts of things went wrong, He was able to pursue His purpose and maintain His character and equilibrium. He did not have to keep changing His mind and would not be deflected from His decision to treat all men and women as brothers and sisters. The nature of the discussion, of course, inevitably turns on the questions raised by the class.

Then, we look at 1 Corinthians 3:10–15 which shows how the image of the house built on a rock was developed by St Paul. Paul and other Christians are like builders who raise up their lives and the life of the church on Christ as the foundation. In this passage fire replaces the storm as the means whereby the building is tested. Moreover, the imagery is further developed so that the reader is asked to make sure that his life built on Christ is made of hard or stable materials and not of such a quality that the trouble represented by fire will destroy it.

(iii) Peter the Fragment

Finally, we see how the name of one of the first apostles was used for a play upon words. He was called Simon, but also given a nickname by Christ. He was called a stone or fragment of rock. In Aramaic, Simon was known as Kephas which means a stone. The name Peter is probably derived from the Greek word *petros* which means a fragment of rock or petra. As a disciple therefore Peter was thought of as being not the rock itself, which was Christ, but a fragment of that rock.

Jesus makes this play upon words in St Matthew 16:13–18 where He says that the Church will be built upon the rock of the faith which Peter has just declared in Jesus. This is a good basis on which to discuss how Peter tried to base his life on Christ's example, so earning the right to be called a fragment of the Rock. It is noteworthy, however, that he is later on called Simon again, when he fails to be as steadfast as his nickname implied (see St Mark 14:37).

Some Useful Hymns
'Rock of Ages', by A. M. Toplady; 'O Safe to the Rock that is Higher than I', by W. O. Cushing; 'Will Your Anchor Hold', by P. J. Owens.

Other Resources
Nelson's Biblical Photographs; Bible Lands Society Slides, Bible Lands Services and Supplies, The Old Kiln, High Wycombe, Bucks.

Historical Note: Outline of the History of Jerusalem
1. Judges 1:21 – an unsuccessful attempt to capture the city at the time of the settlement. This verse is correct in the light of 2 Sam. 5:6–7, and Judges 1:8 is thus wishful thinking!
2. 2 Sam. 5:6–10 and 1 Chron. 11:4–9 – David captures Jebus, renames it Jerusalem and makes it his capital:
   (a) it was well protected, standing on a hill;
   (b) it lay between the north and south of his kingdom;
   (c) it had belonged to no tribe before, being in the hand of the Jebusites, and it was therefore more readily acceptable to all Hebrews than any other site.
3. 1 Kings 6 – Solomon begins the Temple *c.* 959, which took 7 years to build. He took 13 years to build his own palace!
4. Isaiah cs. 36 and 37, duplicated in 2 Kings 18:13–20:19. Sennacherib and the Assyrians ravage Judah (701) and lay siege against Jerusalem, but the siege is unsuccessful. See also Isa. 14:32. In his own records of his campaigns Sennacherib boasted that he had shut up Hezekiah like a bird in a cage. The results show, however, that he could not get the 'bird' out!
5. 2 Kings 24 – First fall of Jerusalem (598/7) and first deportation – Jehoiachim surrenders to the Babylonians. 2 Kings 25: Jer. 52; Zedekiah's revolt (cf. Jer. 27) – Second fall of Jerusalem and its destruction (587/6) by Nebuchadrezzar of Babylon. The siege was begun in January 588 and it took 18 months before lack of food caused the king and some inhabitants to attempt an escape (2 Kings 25:2–4).
6. The Temple rebuilt *c.* 520–515 – Haggai; Ezra cs. 5 and 6. The work of Nehemiah and the rebuilding of the walls of Jerusalem *c.* 437 – Neh. cs. 1–6.
7. Profanation of the Temple – December 167 by Antiochus IV 'Epiphanes' (Syrian overlord); Maccabean revolt; Rededication of the Temple – December 164.

8. 17 B.C. Herod the Great begins the third Temple with fortifications.
9. A.D. 70. Siege and destruction of Jerusalem by the Romans under Titus.

(4) The House of God

'Where does God live?' is a question which most children ask at some point. By the age of 9 years it seems to become very important and so this scheme shows one of the ways in which the question can be tackled.

(a) The Universal House

The aim here is to show that God is thought of as one who lives in the whole of the universe.

(i) The children discuss first of all what we expect to find where God is: truth, goodness, beauty, love, mercy, etc. With the aid of pictures of the galaxies, the countryside, and so on, the class tries to find out where these things seem to be present in the whole realm of nature.

(ii) 1 Kings 8:27 and Psalm 139:8 (simply translate 'Sheol' as the 'underworld' at this stage) can be used to lead up to an understanding of what the Bible means by ' speaking of God as being everywhere. (But cf. Ps. 139 and contrast on Sheol with what is said in Scheme 7 p. 117 below).

(iii) Psalm 104:1–8: Its poetic form is made clear and discussed. From this there should emerge the idea that God is a builder. A useful way of doing this is to duplicate the passage and to search for the references to buildings: *tent, chambers, pillars*. (The passage is also useful as a whole because it is clearly figurative.)

An illustration can be provided such as instanced here, or this can be set as a piece of interpretative art work. (Avoid the traditional picture of the God 'up there' in the sky, because it gives the impression that the Bible was trying unsuccessfully to give a scientific description.)

(b) The Temple

(i) The Miniature Universe
We have to explain that the temples of ancient times were often made to be miniature replicas of the world: Angkor Wat in Cambodia is a famous example. The builders could not make a scale model, but they could represent different ideas about it, one of which was that the world was like a house.

(ii) The Building of the First Temple by Solomon: 1 Kings 5:1–6:38.
The story is told and illustrated to show how Solomon thought of the Temple as a house for God.

(iii) How Jews Felt about the Temple

This was often expressed. Psalm 84 is a useful illustration. It was to them a symbol of the presence of God (cf. the earlier ark of the covenant). On the other hand, we should also note the misunderstanding which the prophets had to resist. This can be done through Jeremiah's attack on the superstition which had grown up round the Temple (Jer. 7:1-4).

The teaching of Stephen in Acts 7:44–50 is then examined to find out how he rejected the Jewish misuse of the Temple, reminding the people that God dwelt in the whole universe. Discussion can follow this on how Christians can fall into the trap of confining God to a church building.

(c) The Body as a House

At this stage we introduce the idea that God is seen to be specially present within the realm of human life and, in Christianity, that He was uniquely present in Jesus of Nazareth.

(i) A recording of 'This Old House' makes a good starting point. We listen to the song and try to discover what house is referred to. This can then be compared to 2 Peter 1:13 where the writer speaks of his body as a tent which must be 'folded up very soon' (Moffatt translation) and to the poem 'My House' by Fay Inchfawn (*Poems*, edited by D. M. Prescott, pp. 92f). The idea of the body as a kind of house in which we live has now been established.

(ii) 1 Cor. 6:12–19; 2 Cor. 6:14–18

The contemporary relevance and validity of Paul's argument that our bodies are a sacred trust can be discussed. The class can make a list of actions which Paul would have included if he had lived today. The list should then be compared with that given in Romans 1:28–31. The books *One For the Road* and *Two For the Road* by Peter Bander, published by Colin Smythe, 1966, 1967, will be found useful in this whole discussion, particularly if the scheme is tried with secondary pupils. The Sermon on the Mount will also be brought into focus through these volumes. The class, then, will be looking for signs of God in human beings: goodness, trustworthiness, and so on.

(iii) Jesus

We now discover these qualities in Jesus in a complete way through a review of some of the stories about Him. Finally, St John 1:14–18 is explored to find the image of the tent and why the writer knows that God's Word was in this particular tent, and we look at St Matthew 26:61; 27:40, 51; St. John 2:20, 21 to find that the temple is now the body of Jesus, i.e. where God is to be found.

(d) The House that Jesus Built

(i) The Word 'House'

The figurative use of the word 'house' is explored in the following ways:
1. looking up and listing the many meanings of the word in a dictionary;
2. making a list as a class exercise;
3. collecting sayings and proverbs in which it occurs.

A text search by the children can then show how the word has many meanings in the New Testament and this may be made easier with the use of workcards. A suitable card could be made along the following lines. At the top could be an instruction telling the children to look up the following passages, find the reference to a house and write down as many facts about it as possible. A suggestion for an illustration to appear on the workcard is given in brackets after each reference.

A. St Matthew 8:14; 11:8; 13:57; 26:26; St Luke 4:38 (illustration: Palestinian House)
B. St Matthew 15:24; St Luke 1:33 (illustration: Jerusalem Temple)
C. St Matthew 12:4 (illustration: Palace)
D. St Luke 1:27; 2:4 (illustration: diagram of family tree of House of David).

In addition the child could be asked to draw a picture or make a model of each kind of house, either copying the picture on the card or drawing the modern equivalent. Finally three questions could be asked.

1. Which of the four groups A, B, C, D are about real buildings?
2. What is different about the building in C?
3. Which group speaks of houses made up of people?

(ii) Jesus the House-builder

The work of Jesus as the builder of a community of people who tried to follow His example is discussed. A list is made of some of the things which Jesus asked of His disciples. Finally, the image of Jesus building the house which is the Church is explored by the use of workcards as given below. In some cases it will be necessary to work through the passages as a class before letting the children work on their own. Some teachers may prefer to use the material in the suggested workcards for ordinary class work. The following poem will also be found useful: 'The Brick' by Michel Quoist, from *Poems* edited by D. M. Prescott, p. 86.

On each of the following suggested workcards, the child is referred to a Bible passage and then asked various questions. Suggestions for illustrations to go with the questions are supplied in brackets where appropriate.

Workcard 1
1 Timothy 3:14–15
a. There are two reasons for the writing of this letter. What are they?
b. What are pillars used for in a building? (illustration: Egyptian Temple).
c. What does the Church support?

d. What is the Church called in this passage?

e. Draw or make a model of an Egyptian or Greek Temple or draw the inside of a church which contains pillars.

Workcard 2

1 Corinthians 3:10–13

a. Who make up God's house? (illustration: group of church members). Illustrate your answer with a symbolic drawing or device.

b. Who laid the foundation as a skilled master builder? (illustration: Foundation)

c. Who is building on the foundation? (illustration: laying of courses of stone on foundation)

d. What do you think 'gold, silver and fine stone' might represent?

e. What do you think 'wood, hay and straw' might represent?

Workcard 3

Ephesians 2:19–22

a. Who form the foundations? (illustration: foundation)

b. What is a corner-stone? (illustration: corner-stone)

c. Who is represented here as the corner-stone?

d. Who holds the building together?

e. What special kind of building is this?

f. Who lives in this building? (illustration of Solomon's Temple with Holy of Holies)

Make a model of this Temple.

Workcard 4

1 Peter 2:4–8

a. Who was the stone rejected by men but chosen by God?

b. Who are to be the stones in the building?

c. What kind of building is it?

d. Who is the corner-stone?

e. Why do men stumble over the corner-stone?

(5) Power and the Spirit

The aim of this scheme is to discover what is meant by spiritual power. Despite what we have maintained in the Introduction and in the previous chapter, in this particular case it is helpful as a preliminary task to examine the different kinds of power we find in the secular world. Nevertheless, it is important to observe that the religious use of the symbol of the Spirit does emerge and religious and moral teaching are given as fully integrated parts of the whole scheme so that the aim is fulfilled.

(a) Power and Representation

(i) Forms of Power

Various kinds of power are listed as they arise out of discussion: water, wind, electricity, gas, muscles, engines, fire, etc. We can usefully divide the different kinds of power into categories: some are visible and others are not; some are natural, while others are made by man employing natural resources.

(ii) Emblems of Power

We find that it is often necessary to indicate the presence of power either because it is being advertised (electricity and gas) or because it is dangerous (power cables, electricity generators).

The children find or are shown some emblems used in advertising or as warning signs. The appropriateness of each emblem is discussed to bring out the fact that an emblem is most effective when it conveys something of the nature of the thing itself, e.g. the zig-zag red line for electricity is taken from lightning – it is red because it is dangerous.

(iii) Other Representations of Power

Records can be used to show how power is indicated in music. The *1812 Overture* by Tchaikovsky, the *Hebrides Overture* by Mendelssohn, Sousa's Marches, 'Mars' from the *Planets Suite* by Gustav Holst, and many others are appropriate.

The artist often wishes to create the impression of power. Numerous paintings are useful for illustrating this. A number of those used in the set of slides called 'War and Peace' (Educational Publications) can be used.

This study of musical and pictorial representations should enlarge the children's idea of power and open up lines of thought which will be useful later. We should note that in this section we are employing what we have said is our main spring-board for the understanding of religious symbols, even though in the scheme as a whole we have allowed ourselves a look at the secular world in general.

(b) Good and Evil Uses of Power

(i) Making Use of Natural Power

The various ways in which we make use of natural power are studied: waterwheels, windmills, dams, nuclear power, solar heating, and so on. We concentrate first on the beneficial uses of power to provide lighting, heating, mobility, medical aid, and the like.

The use of various kinds of power involves the control and direction of different sorts of energy. Examples are the way in which we regulate the flow of water from a dam, steer a car or ship, and control the speed of a train or aeroplane.

This control or direction of energy means that we can use power to help or injure people. Explosives are useful in clearing sites for building or in the construction of roads, for example, but they can also be used to demolish houses and kill those who live in them.

The misuse of power should then be studied to bring out the idea that men and women can themselves be a power for good or evil. Probably the easiest example is that of the use of firearms to indulge in war, hold people in slavery or subjection, and to destroy buildings and crops.

(ii) Christ's Refusal to Use Physical Force

Selections from the gospel story are used here to show how Jesus refused to use physical force because His purpose could not be accomplished in that way: the temptation to rule the world rejected (St Matthew 4:8–10); how He avoided being made a king (St John 6:15); submission to arrest and trial (St John 18:1–8, 33–36); the meaning of Jesus' statement that His kingdom was not of this world (St John 18:36) should be studied and discussed. The class might be asked to describe what sort of kingdom they think Jesus wanted.

(iii) The Effect of Following Jesus

The story of Paul's conversion (Acts 9:1–22) can be used to show the way in which he was changed from a man of hate who wished to kill the Christians to one who spent his life helping people to find a fuller life.

(c) The Symbolism of the Spirit

In this section we look at the ways in which the Spirit has been represented.

(i) The Baptism of Jesus (St Mark 1:9–11)

The Spirit is here compared to a dove. The appropriateness of this symbol for Jesus' attitude is discussed (see p. 114 below).

(ii) Jesus Breathes on the Disciples (St John 20:19–23)

Here it is spoken of as 'breath'. This was a very common way of speaking of the Spirit. Breath stood for life, and so the story suggests that Jesus gave the disciples a new kind of life.

(iii) Pentecost (Acts 2:1–4)

The mighty wind of this story is a symbol for 'the breath of God', while the tongues of fire, recalling the Burning Bush (Exod. 3:1–6) and the burning coal (Isa. 6:6), are suggestive of many things – the Presence of God, the refiner's fire, divine energy, etc. Fire became, in fact, one of the commonest ways of speaking of the spirit.

(iv) The Gifts and Fruit(s) of the Spirit

There are often said to be seven gifts or fruits of the spirit and so the early Christians took over the seven-branched candlestick of Judaism as a representation of the work of the Spirit – see Rev. 1:4; 5:6 and 12; but compare 1 Cor. 12:8–10 and

Gal. 5:22–23, where nine gifts* and nine fruits or qualities or results of possessing the spirit appear to be listed.

It is probably more important here that the pupils should discover for themselves what the gifts and the fruit of Jesus' Spirit might be than to learn any biblical or traditional lists. Consequently, they might be asked to draw a seven-branched candlestick and indicate what each candle or lamp might represent.

Useful Aids
'Pentecost' by El Greco (painting);
'O Thou who camest from above', by C. Wesley, and 'Breathe on me breath of God', by Edwin Hatch (hymns);
'Go it Alone' from 'A Man Dies' (record: 33SX 1609 mono Columbia, EMI Records Ltd), E. Hooper and E. Marvin.

(6) Birds, Men, and God

Through a scheme on birds we can see how they tell us some of the secrets hidden in nature by God, how we try to make use of this knowledge when we find it, and how an appreciation of birds and bird-life leads us to accept a responsible role in our treatment of nature and of living things. Much of the work, therefore, is concentrated on the discovery that there is a message to be found in nature and the need for us to appreciate this.

Work on other curriculum subjects is inevitable in a scheme of this kind. Ideally, the scheme can be worked to cover both nature study and religious education. As this is not always possible, however, the work is set out so that the nature study content is included within the scheme.

Nevertheless, it should be clear that we are not dealing here with a scheme introduced by looking at secular symbols. In the terms of our previous discussion in the preceding chapter we are simply showing how religious symbols are often derived from man's experience of the natural order.

(a) The Wonder of the Bird

The object initially is simply to create a greater awareness of birds, their beauty, the highly adapted structure of their bodies, the mysteries about them which we have still not unravelled and the way in which they have called forth a response from men.

---

* The apparent confusion arises from the fact that two of these gifts, speaking in tongues and interpreting tongues, were not exercised by the apostles until their Pentecost experience described in Acts 2. Other gifts were exercised even by the 70 sent out in the days of Jesus' ministry. The Pentecost experience, however, led to these gifts being exercised more successfully and frequently, both by the 'eleven' and by other Christians after they had undergone their own personal 'Pentecost' experiences.

(i) The Variety of Birds

The subject can be opened up by a study of a number of pictures showing the immense variety of birds. This is immediately followed up by showing how men have reacted to birds, painting pictures of them, writing poetry about them, and making films. Some examples which might be used are: the paintings of Peter Scott; 'To a Skylark', Shelley; 'Ode to a Nightingale', Keats; 'Curlew', Yeats; 'The Thrush's Nest', Clare.

(ii) Bird Song

We play a record (of which a considerable choice is available) of bird song, trying to identify different birds. We note the song of birds is an important part of the country scene. The appearance of the bird in music makes a natural development: 'The Crowing of the Cock' in J. S. Bach's *Matthew Passion*; the bird sounds in the *Toy Symphony* of Leopold Mozart (often wrongly attributed to Haydn); *The Firebird*, Stravinsky. The purpose of bird sounds can be explored further to discover that this is the way the males attract female birds and lay claim to a piece of territory to be used for nesting.

(iii) Bird-Watching as a Hobby

The possibility of making a hobby of bird-watching is explored and some basic information given about the way to go about this. (A number of easily obtainable books give this information.)

(b) Birds and the Secret of Flight

At this stage we discover that some of the mysteries to which scientists have tried to find the answer have been present in the structure of birds and that the advances of science reveal things which were built into the very nature of birds.

(i) Birds in Flight

The structure of a bird's bones, muscles, etc., especially of the wings, are noted, and the mechanics of a bird's ability to fly are analysed. Drawings are used here which the children can copy. The highly developed eyes in birds are discussed and the reasons for them given. The greatest mystery connected with birds is migration and this topic can be pursued. The practice of ringing to plot the flight of birds can be explained, though it must be stressed that this does not tell us why they behave in this way. We also note the extraordinary nature of the bird's ability to find its way over long distances – there have been some recent experiments on this. (Reference can be made to Job 12:7–10; 39:26.)

(ii) Men and Flight

Stories of men watching the flight of birds and attempting to learn the secret of flight can be told: King Bladud, John Damian, Leonardo da Vinci, who all thought that a man could be provided with wings like those of a bird and fly by flapping the wings; Sir George Cayley and Otto Lilienthal who pioneered the making of gliders after the fashion of kites; Orville Wright watched the flight of Buzzards and was inspired to develop the plane: the development of the Spitfire whose inventor, R. J. Mitchell, realized that the aeroplane would be improved by making its wings as one unit with the body of the plane in the manner of a bird's structure. The instruments of an aircraft can be mentioned in addition as complicated attempts to provide planes with the abilities possessed by birds, e.g. radar, etc.

(c) Birds Telling Us Something about God

Having seen that men have still not fully understood the wonderful means at the disposal of the birds, we can understand why men have always been fascinated by them. Because God has always been thought of as the creator, men have felt that the secrets of the birds were also God's secrets. They also found in the bird a way of speaking about God.

(i) Birds Set an Example

The family habits of birds are studied: building and guarding nests; incubating the eggs; shielding nestlings from the sun and keeping them warm; feeding the young. Here we discover how love and care are built into nature. These activities can be seen as examples of the way God wishes us to behave also.

(ii) The Bird as a Symbol for God

The use of the bird as an image for God is not well known but quite prominent in the Bible. Providing the preparatory work already outlined has been done, this can now be appreciated. It is important that we do this as a conscious effort in the appreciation of poetry and so the work is based on Biblical passages.

Deut. 32:11–13; Exod. 19:4–6: The Hebrews think of God taking care of them as being like a bird looking after her brood. The 'poetic licence' should be noted, for we do not know of any birds who actually carry the young on their backs in flight.
Isa. 31:5: God protects Jerusalem like a bird looking after its nest. This can be compared to St Matthew 23:37 where Jesus went to care for the people of Jerusalem like this, but they would not accept His concern for them.
Psalms 17:8; 36:7; 57:1; 61:4; 63:7; 91:4: We note the many times that Hebrew poets thought of God protecting them like a bird casting a shadow over them with its wings.
Mal. 4:2: This verse speaks of the winged sun of righteousness. The sun in Egypt was sometimes pictured with wings because it 'flew' across the sky. In Egypt the sun primarily represented life-giving energy. The Hebrew poet cleverly applies the imagery to the idea of righteousness.
2 Sam. 22:11; Psalm 104:3: Here, God is spoken of as moving on 'the wings of the wind' in order to portray His majesty and all-encompassing presence.
Gen. 1:2: This verse uses a word which suggests that God as creative activity was like a bird brooding over the watery chaos.

(iii) Other Symbolic Uses of Birds

Birds of various kinds have different characteristics which has led to their use in denoting certain kinds of qualities. Two examples are taken to illustrate the point:

1. The Dove: We notice the shape of the dove and the way it flies and behaves. We end with a description of the dove and find that it seems to suggest such things as harmlessness, peace, softness, etc. We turn to St Mark's story of the baptism of Jesus and discuss why the presence of God was described as being like a dove on this occasion (St Mark 1:9–11). We can also note the use of the dove as a symbol of world peace today. We might, in addition, observe the way in which the dove is used symbolically in numerous Christian works of art.

2. The Eagle: This bird is chosen because it shows quite different characteristics. The reasons for the use of the eagle are studied with reference to: 2 Sam. 1:23; Job 39:27–29; Isa. 40:31; as a representation of St John and his gospel; lecterns shaped as an eagle; its use in the national emblems of Germany and the U.S.A.

The possibilities of using other birds as emblems can be explored, the children suggesting what each bird might be used to represent, making a flag or shield using a bird accompanied by a motto.

(d) Preserving the Birds

Care of the birds is something which men have felt they were called upon to do. In this way they have recognized their responsibility as inhabitants of the earth who have the power to destroy or preserve much of the earth's bird life.

(i) The History of Bird Protection

We already find that birds are protected to some extent in biblical times – Deut. 22:6–7 safeguarded the breeding stock, while we find Psalm 84:3–4 speaking of the Temple as a bird sanctuary. (This can be compared to the way birds are protected in the sacred area of the Muslims in Mecca.)

The Christian concern for birds has its roots in the idea that all living things are cared for by God as expressed in St Luke 12:6. We find therefore that the first conservers of bird life were responding to a sense of the beauty and holiness of nature which was a natural expression of their Christian faith. The activities of the Celtic and Anglo-Saxon saints in this connection are as follows:

St Cuthbert who founded the first bird sanctuary in this country on Inner Farne, Northumberland (*c.* 676);

St Columba whose love for birds caused him to become one of the first to become familiar with the passage of migrant cranes. History describes how he succoured a bird for three days on Iona (*c.* 570).

Guthlac who returned to the English fens to live a life somewhat like that of St Francis, close to nature (*c.* 699), and over whose shrine Athelbald built Crowland Abbey.

Serf and Kentigern who are remembered for their love and taming of robins.

Later developments should be noted:

The work of *Gilbert White* (1720–93), a curate of Faringdon, in Hampshire, whose book *The Natural History of Selborne* has been much read.

The Bird Protection Act passed in 1869 due to the work of *Alfred Newton*; its provisions can be noted and the reasons for them explained.

The founding of *The Royal Society for the Protection of Birds* in 1889, from whom further information on this topic is available.

(ii) Our Responsibilities

The idea of the 'balance of nature' is explained at this point with special reference to the part that birds play by eating rodents, insects, the seeds of weeds, etc. On the other hand, we note how men can ruin nesting rounds, pollute the water with oil, etc. This raises the idea that man has a special responsibility.

Some discussion of the misuse of birds by men can be introduced, e.g. cock-fighting and the reasons which led to its abolition. Conservation projects can be outlined in so far as they affect bird-life. Ways in which pupils can participate in this can be explored if only in connection with winter feeding, etc. Finally through discussion, the class can attempt to find out why laws protecting birds have been passed and why great efforts are made by a large number of people to preserve them. It will be quickly seen that it is not simply a matter of self-preservation. Pupils can usually recognize that some people are motivated by a simple love of birds, others by the idea that birds are part of the world which God has entrusted to man's care, and many for both reasons.

(7) The Prophets as Teachers

This scheme is designed to bring out the different ways in which the Old Testament prophets of the eight to the sixth centuries B.C. received their message and the methods they used to get their teaching across to the people. While examining this we learn, of course, a great deal about the content of their teaching, and so an alternative way of tackling this is provided. (For the method as applied to religious education in general cf. pp. 37–38 above, and for both the method and the message of the prophets themselves cf. 'Trees' (c) pp. 93–100 above.)

(a) Lessons from the Past (Amos 2:10 and 3:1–2)

The children can be asked about the stories in the Bible which inform us concerning the incidents mentioned by the prophet. God has shown His love and care for the people. How should the people behave in response to what He has done? How were they behaving? The children can find some of the things the people were doing wrong from Amos 2:6 – the poor who had got themselves into debt were sold as slaves for the debts to be paid – 'a pair of shoes' indicates that the debts were trivial, since the phrase was used as a proverbial expression for something of little value; Amos 2:8 and Isa. 5:11 – drunkenness, even in God's house; the rich pay for their wine from the fines they extract from the poor; Isa.

5:8 – the rich gain as much land and property as possible at the expense of their countrymen – eighth century take-over bids!; Amos 5:12 – bribery and corruption in the courts – the phrase 'in the gate' refers to the fact that all important business, including the execution of justice, was carried out at the city gate.

The result is that their worship is unacceptable to God (Amos 5:21–25; Isa. 1:11–17), and that they will be punished (Isa. 5:25–26, see also Amos' Five Visions in chapters 7–9).

(b) Simple Comparisons Drawn from Everyday Situations

Examine Amos 2:13–16; 5:18–20. The passages both show that there is to be no escape from God. The comparisons in the first passage should be carefully examined: v. 13. A cart laden with the harvest is pressed down in the mud track. vv. 14–16. The four-minute miler will be rooted on the spot! The champion boxer cannot use his strength against God! The bow will not save the archer from the judgment! The most superb horseman will not be able to gallop away! Once these verses have been examined, the children should be able to explain the point of Amos 5:19.

Jer. 18:1–11 should then be examined. It should be observed how Jeremiah makes use of the work of the potter, both to learn what the message is he has to give, and to use as an illustration when he delivers it. From verse 6 the children should be able to state with whom the prophet compares both the potter and the pot. Man's utter dependence on God is shown by the passage.

(c) The Use of a Series of Questions (Amos 3:3–8)

All the questions are drawn from everyday life and they all demand the answer 'No'. Verses 3–6 lead up to the point in verse 7 that just as the answer to these questions is 'No'; in the same way, if we ask whether God acts without warning, the answer is again 'No'. Moreover, in this verse we have a further instance of God's love and care in that He sends the prophets to give the people a chance to repent in time. Verse 8 is also about the prophetic mission. The answer to the first question is 'No one'; in the same way anyone called to be a prophet feels he has no option but to carry out his work (cf. Jer. 1:4–10; Ezek. 2:3–12).

(d) Visions

(i) First, we look at examples of the way in which God speaks to the people through the imaginations of the prophets. It should be observed how the mental pictures themselves are often created out of familiar scenes within the prophet's experiences.

A The Five Visions of Amos

Judgement by Locusts (7:1–3)

Devastation of the crops by locusts was a frequent occurrence. Verse 1 shows that the prophet was influenced by such an attack by the insects in spring. Verse 3 – this judgment is not final. The prophet Joel, at a later period, makes use of this vision (Joel 1:4 and 2:3).

Judgment by Fire (7:4–6)

In the sweltering heat of summer, Amos forecasts a period of exceptional drought. In v. 4 the great deep refers to the mass of water below the flat earth, the source for springs and rivers. This drought is seen as supernatural, since the great deep itself will be dried up and the land will actually burn. v. 6 – the warning being given – God does not carry out this judgment.

The Plumbline (7:7–9)

The builder who tests that his walls are straight is compared with God examining Israel. He finds her wanting, and the judgment is pronounced with an insistence that this time it will indeed be carried out.

A Basket of Summer Fruit (8:1–3)

The chronological sequence of the visions seen as appropriate to certain seasons is completed here at the end of summer. There is a play on words in the Hebrew: 'Summer fruit' and 'end'. The same point, however, is made in any case by the fact that the end of the harvest season is being compared to the end of Israel's days as a nation. Again, there is no hope of the judgment being averted.

A Command to Destroy (9:1–4)

Finally, the prophet sees God Himself commanding that His people should be utterly destroyed. vv. 2–4 emphasize that there is no escape and should be compared with similar passages by the same prophet (see (b) above). 'Sheol' in verse 2 refers to the place of the dead. It does not equal 'hell'. Nevertheless, it was the gloomy place of shades, and the normal belief was that God could not be found there. After death, a man was separated from God (e.g. Pss. 6:5; 115:17.) These verses and Psalm 139:7–12 seem to provide exceptions to the usual belief, but as far as Amos is concerned no comfort is provided, but rather the opposite. Man will never be able to escape God's judgment. Only late in the Old Testament period is there any suggestion of a resurrection or of 'Hell' (Gehenna) (Dan. 12:2; Wisdom 3:1).

A discussion on the social conditions of the eighth century and a consideration of the conditions in our own society, together with the relevance of Amos today, is appropriate at this point. The information gained in section (a) above and by looking at Amos 8:4–6, which is used to show why the visions of judgement were necessary, will provide plenty of material for the discussion. The children can then express the message of Amos for the present day by describing the visions in contemporary terms and using examples from life today: e.g. 'No escape' might be expressed by the idea that infantry facing an army of tanks cannot escape if the only route will take them across a mine field. The visions may be expressed in writing or by an art project, a group collage, or free-expression painting.

B Jer. 1:13–16

A further picture of judgment can be seen from an example in Jeremiah – the boiling cauldron. From verses 14–15 the interpretation of the vision should be clear enough.

Special Note on the 'No Escape' Theme of Amos and on Judgment in General within the Prophets and the Whole Biblical Message (see particularly (b) and (d) above)

Within the discussion suggested in A above, it should be made clear that the harsh messages of judgment were necessary in the eighth–sixth centuries, and are still appropriate today, but that they have to be balanced by the total prophetic message and the teaching of the Bible as a whole. Judgment was and is not God's final word. So that Amos' 'No escape' theology has to be seen in terms of particularly forceful language, employed by the first of the great writing prophets to make a startling impact, while the judgment teaching by the other prophets is balanced by the other side of the coin in their own preaching and writing.

Thus, Hosea preaches the loving-merciful kindness of God (see (f) (i) below), and Isaiah of Jerusalem announces that a remnant of the nation will be saved in the Messianic Age (Isa. 10:20ff and 11:11ff, cf. (g)(i) below); Jeremiah looks forward to the New Covenant being established on men's hearts (Jer. 31:31–34), and Ezekiel to the restoration of the nation after the Babylonian exile (Ezek. 37:1–14 – see (d) (ii) C below), and Ezek. 37:15–28 – see (e) (iv) below); Deutero–Isaiah sees the return of the exiles, which is soon to take place, in terms of the first Exodus experience (Isa. 40:3; 43:18ff), and the Messianic Age that is dawning in terms of comfort and pardon (Isa. 40:1–5); and finally, the same prophet declares that 'many will be accounted righteous' because of the offering of the Suffering Servant (Isa. 53:11 – see (g)(ii) below), who will be a light to the nations groping in the darkness of ignorance, and who will open the eyes of the spiritually blind (Isa. 42:7).

The real fulfilment of these prophetic hopes, of course, is seen in the New Testament, which, while maintaining the judgment theme (the teaching of Jesus Himself containing warnings of judgment – e.g. St Matthew cs. 24 and 25), proclaims the 'Good News' of man's reconciliation with God (Rom. 5:1–11), his healing and restoration (St Mark 2:17; St Luke 15), his salvation without condemnation (Rom. 8:1), through the Incarnate Word (St John 3:16–17), and that the free gift of forgiveness is ever-available to those who would respond (St Luke 23:39–43).

It will be clear from the cross-references to other sections in the scheme that the point made in this note for inclusion in the discussion at this stage will be reinforced as the scheme proceeds. Full discussion of the passages referred to should be left until they are reached in their appropriate context. All that is needed here is that the point is made through a general summary of the total picture and a brief examination of one or two passages, preferably selected from those which do not appear elsewhere in the scheme.

(ii) The Call of Two Prophets

We now see how two prophets received their commission from God through visions.

A *Isaiah of Jerusalem (Isa. 6)*

Isaiah is in the Temple for some great festival occasion. During the service the smoke of the incense suggests to him the train of God's robe and the clouds of heaven, while the singing of the choirs suggest the voices of the seraphim, 'the burning ones' who surround God's throne. Thus inspired, he sees the 'Holiness' of God, i.e. His Glory, Might, Power, and Majesty, and at the same time feels his own unworthiness as a mere man to be in the presence of God. But he knows that whatever praises are going on in the Temple the people are not serving God in their lives, that there is much social injustice and the worship is therefore hollow. In spite of his own unworthiness he is sure he is called by God to deliver His word to the people, and so in his vision he imagines one of the angel-figures coming to him and cleansing him, the cleansing being expressed by the symbol of the burning coal.

B *Ezekiel (Ezek. 1)*

Similarly, Ezekiel at his call sees a vision of the glory of God. It is possible to give detailed interpretations for many of the images in the vision, but in this scheme it is probably better to say that all these images and to us, weird descriptions, are simply Ezekiel's way of attempting to convey something of the glory of God, the transcendent majesty of the Lord, which so overwhelmed him, Ezekiel himself knowing that man cannot describe God. The guarded language of v. 28 should be noted: 'Such was the appearance of the likeness of the glory of the Lord'.

Having examined both of these passages, the children should express their own idea of the glory of God through an art form. In the case of painting or collages a vivid use of colour and shape is indicated. Images, whether from the imagination or taken up from one of the passages, should be indistinct, e.g. if a seraph were required, a few lines indicating a wing shape would be sufficient. Thus, the children through their own expression work would be taught the 'feel' of the guarded language, the true spirit of the use of literary symbolism.

C *Further Examples*

Ezek. 37:1–14 – 'The Valley of Dry Bones' – a vision of the restoration of the nation. There is no suggestion of personal resurrections.

Ezek. 40:1–48:35 – Vision of the restored Temple.

(e) Acted Symbols

The teaching of the prophets was sometimes given in a more dramatic way. Comparisons can be made with games in which a group guess what is being portrayed through a mime and with plays that convey the author's message for his time. The examples given below should be examined and the children should be able to discover the meaning behind each acted symbol:

(i) Jer. 19
The breaking of the pot – total destruction for Jerusalem; historical fulfilment 586 B.C.

(ii) Jer. cs. 27 and 28
The sign of the yoke – Judah taken by Babylon, 598–586 and exile to 538.

(iii) Ezek. cs. 4 and 5
Descriptions of the coming siege of Jerusalem and the exile.

A   *Ezek. 4:1–3*
The siege; tile – a brick, dried by the sun with a relief drawing of Jerusalem under siege.

B   *Ezek. 4:4–8*
Symbol of the number of years Israel and Judah respectively are to suffer punishment. Some scholars doubt whether Ezekiel would actually have performed this sign as given, but suggest the sign has been emphasized by the dramatic form being applied to the literature.

C   *Ezek. 4:9–17*
Verse 9 – mixed grains suggest a scarcity of food in exile, as does the measuring in verses 10 and 16. Verse 13 – the people will be reduced to cooking food in an unclean way – they will not be able to keep to the regulations of the Law.

D   *Ezek. 5*
Military defeat and deportation of the people.

(iv) Ezek. 37:15–28
The two sticks. Ezekiel is thinking of an ideal situation after restoration of the nations Israel and Judah. Because of the continuing hatred between the Jews and the Samaritans in the post-exile period, this sign was not fulfilled historically.

The Jeremiah examples and the idea behind Ezekiel 5 could be expressed most appropriately through dance-mime activity, thought out and created by the children themselves.

(f) Life's Experiences

Here, we are concerned with occasions when prophets have learnt what they have to teach the people from experiences in their own personal lives, and how, in turn, they made use of these experiences to get their message across.

Reference can first be made to experiments which show how animals learn by experience, and then examples from everyday life can be used to show how we all learn from what happens to us in our own lives.

(i) Hosea cs. 1–3, particularly 3:1ff
Just as Hosea took his wife back, in fact, had to buy her back out of slavery, so God will again show His steadfast love and forgive Israel.

(ii) Jer. 16:1–13
Jeremiah is instructed not to marry, as a sign to the people of the bad time to come – an inappropriate time for setting up house. Both these cases, of course, provide further examples of acted symbols.

(g) Poetic Figures

The prophets pronounced God's judgment, but they also gave the people hope. Isaiah of Jerusalem (who was responsible for the teaching of cs. 1–39 of the book that bears his name) expressed this hope in two ways: first, God would send a Messiah, i.e. the Anointed One, a great king; and second, a remnant of the people would be saved from whom the new nation would grow (10:20–23). The second Isaiah (Deutero-Isaiah), who lived during the exile in Babylon (cs. 40–55), also gives a picture of the Messianic Age (e.g. c. 40), but, in addition, gives us four songs concerning another figure, the Servant of the Lord.*

(i) The Messiah

A *Isa. 7:14*
A young married woman (as the Hebrew actually implies) will have a son and will give him the name Immanuel, as a sign of the better days ahead. All Hebrew names have a meaning or signify something. In this case, Immanuel = 'God with us'. All Isaiah is saying is that the name of this child is to show that God will again dwell with His people, and the birth of the boy will announce that the new age will come, as soon as the present troubles of Ahaz' reign pass (i.e. the threat of war with Ephraim (Israel) and Syria and all that this would mean).

B *Isa. 9: 6–7 (RSV)*
'For to us a child is born, to us a son is given . . .': Note the Hebrew poetic style of repeating the same statement in two different ways.
'And his name will be called Wonderful Counsellor"†: As people had come to

* Since the Servant is an anointed figure (Isa. 42:1), he is Messianic in the overall sense of the term, but in our view is not to be identified with the Davidic kingly Messiah, despite Helmer Ringgren *Messiah in the Old Testament*, SCM Press, 1955, ch. 6, pp. 65ff. The two concepts come together for the first time in Jesus and Peter found this particularly difficult as the incident at Caesarea Philippi shows (Mark 8:32–33 and parallels). To avoid confusion we reserve the word 'Messiah' for the Davidic kingly concept.

† OUP editions of RSV (cf. and contrast the majority of English editions) keep the American spelling with a single 'l'.

the kings for counsel and advice for the settling of disputes, etc., (cf. 2 Sam. 15:1–6 where Absalom makes a claim for the throne by taking over this function from his father, David, and 1 Kings 3:16–18), so they would now come to the Messiah for his judgment and help.

'Mighty God': 'Mighty in battle'. He will do mighty deeds. Initially the Messiah will need to re-establish the kingdom by defeating the oppressors of Israel and Judah. As David had established the empire, so the Messiah would re-establish it. There is, however, a further thought implied. As the kings had been adopted as sons of God, each on the day of his enthronement and invested with God's power and authority to administer His Law (the code of the Sinaitic covenant) (Ps. 2:7), so the Messiah will be designated as God's son.

'Everlasting Father': The Messiah will always be as a father to his people. His care for them will be constant and unfailing. 'Everlasting' may also indicate that the new rule will not cease, for there will always be sons to succeed the Messiah, who will carry on his rule of prosperity and peace.

'Prince of Peace': Once the kingdom is re-established (cf. verse 7), the Davidic Messiah (cf. verse 7 again) will be a Prince of Peace. His sword can be laid aside once and for all. Wars will cease (cf. Isa. 2:4) and all will be contented.

C *Isa. 11:1–9*

Verse 1: 'Stock of Jesse' – Jesse was David's father. This passage then is again about the Davidic Messiah.

Verse 2: No man can do God's work without the Spirit of God helping him (cf. the descent of the Spirit upon the Judges – Judges 3:10; 6:34; 11:29; 13:25; 14:6; 14:19; 15:14; and upon the apostles in Acts 2). The Messiah will be granted the gifts necessary to exercise his rule in the way God wants him to rule.

Verses 3 and 4: He will not judge on appearances. With God's help, he will have a true understanding of people's problems and situations. The bad social conditions of the eighth to the sixth centuries will not recur. (For Isaiah himself understand this in terms of the eighth century only, and our extension in terms of the post-exilic reinterpretation.)

Verses 6–9: A poetic hyperbole – the idea of different animals, which are normally enemies, eating and sleeping together, implies three ideas:

1. The thought of verses 3–5 is carried on. The rich and poor will live together in the Messianic Age happily. There will be no more oppression of the poor, indeed, the distinction between the rich and the poor will disappear, for there will be enough for all.
2. Nations that have been at war against each other will now live peaceably, side by side. There is probably an allusion to Assyria in the 'lion' and the 'bear', but in the light of later history, we might suggest the verse implies for us, as for the people of the exilic and post-exilic periods, that both Assyria and Babylon, once oppressors of Israel and Judah, respectively, are to be at peace with God's people, represented by the 'lamb' and the calf', though for Isaiah himself, Assyria was uppermost in his mind, as chapter 10 shows.
3. A return to an ideal state, a new paradise, is promised.

Discussion: A class discussion can examine to what extent Jesus was like the Messiah described by the Book of Isaiah, finding similarities to the points raised. Further we can explore the question as to how far the prophet's hopes for a world peace and goodwill and for social equality or justice have been achieved, what part Christianity has played in this, and what still remains to be done.

(ii) The Servant of the Lord

In the Servant Songs of 2 Isaiah the prophet speaks of the faithful Jews within Israel as though they were one man acting on behalf of the whole nation. The picture of the servant is therefore a poetic device. Each song is taken in turn and the images or metaphors used are detected and explained.

A *Isa. 42:1–4* God speaks

The Servant is chosen and equipped by God to bring a right way of living to the world. This will be carried out, not by violence, but by quiet witness and perseverance. His actions rather than his words will speak and those who are at the point of despair will not be 'kicked while they are down'.

B *Isa. 49:1–6* The Servant speaks

The same theme is pursued and developed. Note the new metaphors: his mouth is like a sharp sword – when it is right to speak, he does so convincingly and his words show the evil in the lives of the people; he is a polished arrow – he goes straight to the point.

C *Isa. 50:4–9* The Servant speaks again

Further images are used: he is scourged and mocked – the true Israel will have to suffer many things; he sets his face like a flint – the mission will be carried out steadfastly with no wavering of purpose; the servant puts his case before God to be judged, with confidence in his innocence.

D *Isa. 52:13–53:12*

52:13–15 God and *53:1–9* the nations speak

Ultimately, the Servant, the ideal Israel within Israel, will be vindicated before the rulers of the earth. He has been despised and rejected like a plant growing in poor soil, but God has cared for him. When these Jews suffered, others self-righteously thought that God was punishing them, but the truth was that their suffering was vicarious, i.e. for others including those who mocked them; indeed, it was on behalf of the whole world. He was shunned as a leper, and then condemned, as in a court, by the world and punished – yet he was innocent.

53.10–12 The prophet comments and God replies

The Servant's suffering is part of God's plan for the people. After his death he will be seen to have been innocent and will be remembered with gratitude and fully vindicated.

Discussion: Again it is possible to compare the Servant with Jesus and certainly this is what the early Christian church did. In this case the class will search for incidents in the life of Christ which make Him a fulfilment of these prophecies.

Another approach is to remain within the Jewish framework in which the songs were originally composed and to consider how the Jewish nation has often fulfilled the prophecies of Deutero-Isaiah. The class would need to discover how much Jews have given to the world – they are usually surprised to find how many of the great musicians, writers, and scientists have been Jews. The way in which the Jews have been persecuted – and still are – is well known, but the reasons for this are often misunderstood. A discussion along these lines can do much to encourage mutual understanding and also make up in a little measure for the part which Christians have played in the harrying of the Jews.

(8) Water

In this final example,* we again see how a natural element has been employed as a rich religious symbol to convey spiritual truths.

(a) Introduction

The children can suggest the ways in which water is used and give examples of its dangers:

(i) All living things need water to survive.
(ii) Water is also used for cleansing purposes.
(iii) On the other hand, it can also be a threat to life – men have always feared floods; sea-faring has always been a dangerous occupation; the rules for safe bathing at the sea-side and in rivers must be strictly observed if tragedies from bathing are to be averted.

The teacher should then indicate how from these experiences in everyday living it is not surprising that water has been employed as a religious symbol:

(i) for the essential spiritual needs of man; and
(ii) as a symbol of spiritual cleansing; while
(iii) in other contexts it is seen as a symbol of destructive power, of imminent death, often described in terms of the place where the demons, dragons, etc., dwell.

(b) Waters of Life

We begin by looking at water as a symbol of life. The children can look up each passage and suggest with help where necessary what the symbol implies in each case.

* By way of preparation a useful story for infant classes is 'God's Gift of Water' by Ruth de Villiers, from *Further Tales to Tell to Little Children* by Elsie Helena Spriggs and others, Religious Education Press, 1944, Pt. III, pp. 98ff.

(i) Gen. 2:10

A river waters the Garden of Paradise; at the beginning of the myth Man is at one with God and the rest of creation.

(ii) Ps. 42:1

As the deer longs for flowing streams, so the psalmist longs for God, cf. St Matthew 5:6, and also Ps. 23:2. Note how a hard fact of life – the scarcity of water in the dry season in Palestine – heightens the symbolic image.

(iii) Isa. 55:1

God's grace cannot be purchased. The whole passage Isa. 55:1–13 is a hymn of joy and triumph at Israel's coming restoration. Verses 10–11 – as rain causes growth and fruit, so does God's word.

(iv) Isa. 58:11

Water – a symbol of God-given strength.

(v) Ezek. 47:1–12

The waters of life for a new paradise, cf. Joel 3:18; Zech. 14:8; Rev. 22.

(vi) St John 4:1–15

Living water – Jesus gives God's life – the nourishment for the relationship between God and Man (cf. (i), (iii), and (v) above).

In each of these cases the physical essential is symbolic of man's spiritual essentials. There are opportunities here for art work, the children showing through painting or some other medium something of the significance of the symbol of water as offering life. It is desirable that the art work is itself symbolic in character and not 'photographic', as it were. For example, a picture of a river flowing through the countryside on a summer's day is not enough for the purpose of the children entering into the spirit of expressing themselves symbolically. It would be better for them to create or devise a motif such as having a fountain in the centre which is surrounded by a complete ring of flowers, perhaps with other plants, or other living things, without either earth or sky automatically needing to be represented.

The teacher can also direct the class to look at these further passages, but will need to give the explanation himself.

(vii) St John 21:1–14

Once Jesus as Lord of Creation has controlled the elements, and the sea particularly (cf. (d) below) – St John 6:16–21 cf. St Matthew 14:22–27; St Mark 6:45–51 and 4:35–41 – cf. St Matthew 8:18, 23–27; St Luke 8:22–25 – then the water becomes the source of an abundant harvest.

(viii) St John 2:1–11

A different use – the water becomes wine – the faith of Judaism gives place to the gospel in the New Creation.

(ix) St John 3:5

Birth into the new order is through the sacrament of baptism. Partaking in the rite itself, however (water), is not enough, as St Paul shows by comparing the corresponding acts in the Old Testament exodus-wilderness experiences (1 Cor. 10:1–5), but a man must receive the Spirit (cf. 1 Cor. 2:10ff).

(c)   Water for Cleansing

In this section the teacher will probably need to expound each text. This should be followed up, however, by a workcard on the texts to ensure the children have grasped and really understood the points made.

(i) Ritual washing of garments – Exod. 19:10; Lev. 14:8 and 47.

(ii) Ritual washing of self – Lev. 14:8; 2 Kings 5:1–14.

(iii) Symbolic use in poetry of this idea, transformed to washing away sin: Ps. 51:2; Isa. 1:16. Compare the lustrations of the Qumran Sect, the Dead Sea community and of the Essenes as a whole.

(iv) John's baptism of repentance – new element – a once and for all washing – St Matthew 3:6; St Mark 1:5; St Luke 3:3; St John 1:26, 28, 31.

(v) Outward washing in itself, however, is not enough, but it can be a symbol of a spiritual reality (cf. (b)(iii) above). The precise form of the ritual is not important, St John 13:3–10; Heb. 10:22; 1 Pet. 3:21; cf. St Luke 11:39.

(d)   Waters of Destruction

The Hebrews, like other Semites, always feared the sea (cf. Ps. 107:25–29) and large lakes. In them the great dragon, Leviathan, and the crocodile (theriomorphic expressions of evil demons) lurked. The imagery reflects the watery-chaos of Babylonian mythology, which was also reflected in the Priestly account of Creation in Genesis 1.

Again, the teacher will have to take the initiative if this symbol is not to be misunderstood. There is, however, a further opportunity for art work. In addition, the hymns 'Eternal Father strong to save' and 'Will your anchor hold in the storms of life?' will be useful, and the passage in (ii) below could provide the basis of a dance-drama.

(i) Ps. 69:1–2

The psalmist fears being overwhelmed by enemies. The language of these verses is metaphorical.

(ii) St Mark 4:35–41 (cf. St Matthew 8:15, 23–27; St Luke 8:22–25)

In Mark, Jesus speaks to the sea or waves as if speaking to demons – lit. 'Be muzzled!' (RSV 'Peace, be still!'). The Lord of Creation overcomes the forces of evil (cf. also St Mark 6:45–51 and St John 21:1–14, (b) above). In each synoptic gospel the story of the calming of the storm is followed by Legion being cast out of the Gerasene Demoniac (St Mark 5:1–19; St Matthew 8:28–34; St Luke 8:26–39). Observe that the demons, through the swine, are sent back to the place of demons, the sea, where they can do no further harm, for Jesus has already controlled their domain.

(iii) Rev. 13:1–10

Here, the Roman Empire is likened to a beast incited by Satan (the dragon), which rises out of the sea (verse 1) to persecute the saints or Christ's followers. But this provides an opportunity for their encouragement and gaining strength, for salvation is through following the Lamb who redeems them (Rev. 14:4), and gives them a chance to show their trust in God, the Creator of earth, sea, and the fountains of water (Rev. 14:7).

(e) Conclusion

The destructive power of water, however, is not always to be feared. Indeed, to gain new life (cf. (b) above) it is essential to pass through the waters of death. Just as Jesus calmed the storm, so that the sea became a place of abundance, so similarly, at the beginning of the gospel, at His baptism, He had crossed His Sea of Reeds and risen up out of the water, thus prefiguring that through His death on the cross He would overcome evil and in leaving the tomb rise again to new life (cf. Gen. 1:2, 6–7 – the watery chaos is subdued in order that the creation can take place). Furthermore, St Paul sees that the Christian must follow this procedure (Rom. 6:4), the new life, however, being available within this present life.

We can also consider the similar use of imagery – concerning the River Jordan as the river of death to be crossed before Heaven can be reached – in the first verse of the negro spiritual 'Swing Low, Sweet Chariot', where the journey across the river means release from the 'living' death of slavery.

Finally, it is important to note how the significance of water as a symbol in baptism changes according to the argument of a particular context. In St John 3:5 we saw that water here symbolizes the gift of new life, as in St John 4. In Romans 6:4 the water represents death and evil to be overcome. In St John 13:3–10 and 1 Peter 3:21 water is seen as a cleansing agent. (cf. 1 Cor. 6:11).

The scheme could appropriately conclude therefore with a discussion on how throughout life we have to overcome the waters of death by cleansing our lives to receive the waters of life. The tensions and problems of modern living in spiritual and psychological terms would provide the material for this.

Select Bibliography

(a) Religious Education (General)

Schools Council: *Religious Education in Secondary Schools*, Working Paper 36, Evans/Methuen, 1971

M. Grimmitt: *What Can I Do in RE?, Guide to Modern Approaches*, Mayhew-McCrimmon, 1973

Journal (CEM): *Learning for Living, A Journal of Religious Education* (formerly *A Journal of Christian Education*), Christian Education Movement, Annandale, 2 Chester House, Pages Lane, London, N10 1PR

(b) Religion and Religious Education and the Arts

V. R. Bruce and J. D. Tooke: *Lord of the Dance, An Approach to Religious Education*, Pergamon, 1966

H. Elfick: *Folk and Vision Book of Readings*, Rupert Hart-Davies Educational Publications, 1971

George Ferguson: *Signs and Symbols in Christian Art* (300 illus.), OUP, 1954, 1st paperback 1961

Sid. G. Hedges (ed.): *With One Voice*, REP (Pergamon Group), 1970

C. Herbert: *The New Creation, A Dramatic Approach for Integrated Studies*, REP, 1971

E. Newton and W. Neil: *The Christian Faith in Art* (219 illus.) (designed by George A. Adams), Hodder & Stoughton 1966 (particularly valuable for theological insights from art)

T. H. Parker and F. J. Teskey (compilers): *Let There Be God*, REP (Pergamon Group), 1968

K. P. Roadley: *Travellers: Symbol in Story*, Edward Arnold, 1977

D. Whittle: *Christianity and the Arts*, A. R. Mowbray & Co. Ltd, 1966

For other relevant books on Dance see p. 16 note 4 above.

Articles in *Learning for Living* (see (a) above):

L. Atherton: 'Drama. Work in a Primary School', a report on the use of Norse legends, Vol. 7, No. 5, May 1978, pp. 17ff

J. R. Bailey: 'Folk Song in the RE Lesson', Vol. 7, No. 4, March 1968, pp. 19ff

J. Boyce: 'Music', Vol. 9, No. 2, Nov. 1969, pp. 18ff

G. Brooke: 'Religious Studies Through Art', Vol. 14, No. 2, Nov. 1974, p. 56 and pp. 65ff
V. Bruce: 'Dance and Drama, Language for Primary School Children', Vol. 10, No. 3, Jan. 1971, pp. 23ff
T. Jasper: 'Pop – The New Way of Living', Vol. 9, No. 4, March 1970, pp. 18ff
T. Jasper: 'The Big Six', Vol. 10, No. 4, March 1971, pp. 25ff
R. W. Street: 'The Use of Poetry in Religious Education', Vol. 8, No. 4, March 1969, pp. 11ff
 For material on specific themes see suggestions given for examples in chapter 2 above.

(c) World Religions

General and Approach
Sid. G. Hedges (ed.): *With One Voice* (see (b) above)
S. A. Nigosian: *World Religions*, Edward Arnold, 1977
Geoffrey Parrinder: *Worship in the World's Religions*, Faber and Faber, 1961
K. P. Roadley: *Questing. Symbol in World Religions*, Edward Arnold, 1977
N. Smart: *The Religious Experience of Mankind*, Fontana, 1971

Islam
K. Cragg: *The House of Islam*, Dickenson (California), 1975
D. James: *Islamic Art, An Introduction*, Hamlyn, 1974

Judaism
M. Domnitz: *Judaism*, Ward Lock Educational, 1970
H. Wouk: *This is my God*, Fontana, 1976

Sikhism
W. Owen Cole: *A Sikh Family in Britain*, REP, 1973
W. Owen Cole and Piara Singh Sambhi: *Sikhism*, Ward Lock Educational, 1973

Hinduism
J. Hinnels and E. Sharpe: *Hinduism*, Oriel Press, 1972
Yorke Crompton: *Hinduism*, Ward Lock Educational, 1970

Buddhism
E. Zürcher: *Buddhism*, Routledge and Kegan Paul, 1962
W. MacQuitty: *Buddha*, Nelson, 1969

Resources
 (i) Centres specifically concerned with Religious Education:
  RE Resources Centre, Westhill College, Birmingham, B29 6LL
  RE Resources Centre, Borough Road College, Isleworth, Middlesex
 (ii) Commission for Racial Equality, Elliott House, 10–11 Allington Street, London SW1E 5EH for

'SHAP' Working Party Publication *World Religions — Aids for Teachers* — an essential booklist.
The Religious Studies Department at Borough Road College will provide information about SHAP courses for teachers and lecturers.

(d) Religious Language

F. W. Dillistone (ed.): *Myth and Symbol*, SPCK, 1966
F. W. Dillistone: *Christianity and Symbolism*, Collins, 1955
M. Eliade: *Myth and Reality*, Harper and Row, 1963
T. Fawcett: *The Symbolic Language of Religion*, SCM Press, 1970
T. Fawcett: *Hebrew Myth and Christian Gospel*, SCM Press, 1973
S. H. Hooke: *Alpha and Omega, A Study in the Pattern of Revelation*, Nisbet, 1961
Keith McWilliams: *The Language of Religion* (pack of notes and sets), Edward Arnold, 1976
I. T. Ramsay: *Religious Language*, SCM Press, 1957
K. P. Roadley: *Travellers: Symbol in Story* (see (b) above) and *Questing: Symbol in World Religions* (see (c) above)
See also: *The Pelican Gospel Commentaries*: D. E. Nineham, *Saint Mark*, 1963; J. C. Fenton, *Saint Matthew*, 1963; G. B. Caird, *Saint Luke*, 1963; John Marsh, *Saint John*, 1968; Penguin Books Ltd (now published by SCM Press, 1978)

(e) Versions of the Bible

A. T. Dale: *New World, The Heart of the New Testament in Plain English*, OUP, 1967, and *Winding Quest, The Heart of the Old Testament in Plain English*, OUP, 1972
Both these deliberately designed for young people with vocabulary for 9 plus age ranges, well illustrated. See also the same author's *The Bible in the Classroom*, OUP, 1972
Revised Standard Version
New English Bible, OUP and CUP

List of Examples

Section Three Introducing Literary Religious Symbols

Index